WALTZING INTO WAR

War against Napoleon is hours away.

A French spy joins the British Army's finest at a Ball in Brussels.

He is Brigadier-General Charles de la Bédoyère,

a combination of the real d'Artagnan and the fictitious Richard Sharpe:

fearless, famous and foolish.

How Britain almost
lost the Battle of Waterloo by

Waltzing into War

Roger Macdonald

THE GOODCHILD PRESS
LONDON   WASHINGTON DC   OSLO

First published 2015 by
THE GOODCHILD PRESS LIMITED
Reg.Off: Redwoods, 2 Clystworks Clyst Road Topsham Exeter Devon EX3 0DB
email: publisher@thegoodchildpress.co.uk

By the same author:
The Queen's Diamonds
The Man in the Iron Mask

A CIP catalogue record for this book
is available from the British Library.
ISBN 978 1 897657 00 3

Set in Garamond 13pt on 15.8
Book design by Simon Smale
Dust jacket by Peter Hawksley, Christopher Meakin and the author
All illustrations are taken from the author's private collection

Printed and bound in Great Britain
by Short Run Press Limited
25 Bittern Road, Exeter, Devon EX2 7LW

CONTENTS

For Jeannie, *who loves to dance*

Adapted from a talk given by the author
to an invited audience at the Victoria & Albert Museum
during an exhibition on 19th century Viennese history and
culture in the V&A's series on Style Cities

Author's Introduction

The unlikely combination of Hollywood and Napoleon sparked my interest in the evolution of the waltz. It was a continental invention which scandalised British society yet featured four times on ladies' dance cards at the most famous ball in history. The Duchess of Richmond's Ball, held in Brussels just before the Battle of Waterloo, was unique. Not only were some of the British officers on the dance floor about to die violently on the battlefield, but unknowingly a French spy lurked in their midst.

My history tutor at Hertford College Oxford, Felix Markham, wrote a biography of Bonaparte which broke fresh ground, making use of many original sources. So he became the natural choice for film director Stanley Kubrick to be his consultant on an epic movie he planned about the life of Napoleon for MGM.

Kubrick summoned us both to his home in Hertfordshire, where we met eager executives from Warner Brothers. Felix announced our dramatic discovery (at that stage little more than unsubstantiated if persistent hearsay) that a French general called la Bédoyère had audaciously mingled with the British officers waltzing at the eve of battle ball. Throughout the meeting with Kubrick and his advisers, Felix Markham clutched close to his chest an impressively thick file marked 'Brussels Spy'. Only afterwards did I learn that the file contained only one document, a bill for a most indulgent meal in a Brussels restaurant, plus dozens of blank sheets of headed paper from Hertford College Oxford.

Long before crowd scenes could be generated by computer graphics, Stanley Kubrick planned to hire 50,000 Rumanian soldiers, each dressed in an historically accurate uniform, to represent Napoleon's grand army. Eventually the escalating budget proved too much for MGM to swallow, even for the distinguished director of *Spartacus* and the *2001: A Space Odyssey*. The project was duly abandoned.

Later Kubrick attempted unsuccessfully to revive 'Napoleon' with United Artists, telling them as little as possible about the project, except that he planned to make 'the best movie ever'. Unsurprisingly, the bean counters did not believe him.

Shortly before his death, Felix Markham handed me a vast collection of nineteenth century historical artwork and photographs. For many years afterwards it gathered dust in my loft, together with the dog-eared file marked 'Brussels Spy'. Then a project for the Victorian and Albert Museum prompted me to retrieve the file, which much to my surprise no longer contained nothing but blank pages. Rather, there was a copy of a handwritten letter from Aubrey Hepburn to Kubrick from her home near Geneva, regretfully turning down the role of Napoleon's first wife, Josephine.

The file also contained a screenplay for 'Napoleon' written by Kubrick himself; and Kubrick's final pitch to United Artists. Most important of all, it contained the outcome of long-forgotten research by Felix and myself into the elusive Charles de la Bédoyère, including letters from his family and extracts from unpublished Flemish sources. I still like to imagine that our joint efforts, whose fruits appear in this volume, would have helped Stanley Kubrick make that best-ever movie.

Any book must have its enthusiastic champions if it is to appear in print. My special thanks are due to my publishers Goodchild, in particular to Chris Meakin and Peter Hawksley, for taking on such an ambitious project against the clock and making many helpful suggestions and improvements; to Short Run Press of Exeter, especially to Mark Couch and Simon Smale, for demonstrating that speed and skill can go hand-in-hand in a fine example of book production and design.

Simon Macdonald carried out the complex task of converting old pictures into pixels and once again rescued my computer from complete collapse. It has been a family effort, in which Tim Macdonald, a former history scholar at Brasenose College, highlighted numerous shortcomings in the text. My wife Jeannie has been magnificently tolerant of the organised pandemonium which alone has made it possible to publish this book on the 200th anniversary of the Duchess of Richmond's life-changing ball.

Roger Macdonald
Richmond- upon-Thames
June 2015

Kubrick's epic on the life of Napoleon was never made but the research for the film unearthed clues to the identity of the French spy at the pre-Waterloo ball

The site of what would become Hertford College, Oxford, in the Napoleonic period.
Of only slightly more recent vintage was Hertford's original telephone switchboard,
positioned above the college porter's bed. Director Stanley Kubrick, planning an epic movie
on Napoleon, called from Los Angeles in a failed attempt to speak to Napoleonic expert
Felix Markham (a Hertford don) in the middle of the night. The conversation that ensued
was reminscent of Tom Sharpe's satirical novel on Oxbridge, Porterhouse Blue

Chronology

1750   First mention of the waltz in Vienna

1765   Almack's Assembly Rooms, hub of London society, opens its ballroom (February)

1766   Haydn composes first known waltz for piano

1769   Wellington born (May); Napoleon born (August)

1773   Royal balls in Vienna are thrown open to commoners

1789   The Duke of Richmond fights royal duke in duel (May); Storming of the Bastille heralds French Revolution (July)

1791   Mozart composes music for carnival ball in Vienna

1794   Queen Consort of Prussia bans 'scandalous' waltz

1798   Napoleon reads of romantic waltzes under the shadow of the Pyramids

1804   Napoleon crowns himself Emperor (December)

1805   Wellington and Nelson meet (September), seven weeks before the Battle of Trafalgar

1806   The Continental System bans British trade with Europe

1808   Spanish rising against France (May); Wellington sails to Lisbon and takes command in the Peninsula Campaign

1809   British Cabinet ministers Castlereagh and Canning fight a duel (September)

1812   Austrian diplomat arranges the first waltz at Almack's; Napoleon's disastrous retreat from Moscow (October-December)

1814   Napoleon abdicates and is exiled to Elba (May); the Congress of Vienna decides little about Europe but does a lot of dancing

1815   Napoleon escapes from Elba (February) and returns to power (March); following the Duchess of Richmond's ball in Brussels, Wellington wins the Battle of Waterloo (June); Napoleon abdicates again and is exiled to St. Helena (October)

1821   Napoleon dies on St. Helena (May)

1822   Castlereagh commits suicide (August)

1852   Wellington, while commander-in-chief of the British Army, dies (September)

1867   Johann Strauss II composes his famous waltz, On the Beautiful Blue Danube. Its first performance is a flop

Dramatis Personae
(which they certainly were…)

Alexander Pavlovich, Alexander I, Russian Czar
Loose cannon who finds meeting the common people a chastening experience

Bathurst, Benjamin
Ambitious young diplomat whose importance lies only in his mysterious disappearance

Castlereagh, Viscount, Robert Stewart
Dexterous politician hiding dark secrets

Holland, Lady, Elizabeth Vassall Fox
Society outcast whose foreign policy trumps that of the British Government

Jersey, Countess of, Sarah Villiers
Self-appointed Queen of London society with a closet full of skeletons

La Bédoyère, Charles de
Dashing French soldier who takes one chance too many

Metternich, Prince Clemens von
Power broker of Europe, whose career comes to a penniless end beside the English seaside

Napoleon Bonaparte
Charismatic French Emperor whose famous luck finally runs out

Richmond, Duchess of, Charlotte Lennox
Irascible, domineering: a match for the Duke of Wellington

Richmond, Duke of, George Lennox
Prickly dolt who dies a terrible death

Talleyrand, Prince Charles-Maurice
Supreme exponent of self-interested diplomacy

Twysden, Reverend Philip
Convivial Anglican bishop by day, cunning highwayman by night

Wellington, Duke of, Arthur Wellesley
War hero and womaniser

Chapter One

Duel at Dawn

EVEN MINUTES AFTER SUNRISE, at six a.m. on Thursday 21 September 1809, two carriages came to a halt at the obelisk on London's Putney Heath. Their occupants were scrupulously punctual, as befitting two gentlemen bent upon shooting at one another in a duel. What made this clandestine rendezvous more unusual than most was that it occurred in the midst of Great Britain's life-or-death struggle against Napoleon Bonaparte and involved two members of the Cabinet: Robert Stewart, Viscount Castlereagh, the Secretary at War, had called out George Canning, the Foreign Secretary.

The morning mist took more than half an hour to clear. Canning sat quietly in his coach. Castlereagh walked calmly up and down, humming tunes he had heard at the opening of the Royal Opera House in Covent Garden, three nights earlier. He was known to be a crack shot, with his own set of duelling pistols, while Canning had never fired pistol in his life. The previous evening, Canning had a written a final letter to his wife Joan, fully expecting, he confessed grimly, at best to make her a 'proud widow'. In the circumstances, his choice of a second, his friend and Member of Parliament George Ellis, was not ideal. Ellis's hands were shaking so much that Castlereagh's own second, Francis Seymour-Conway, the notoriously debauched Lord Yarmouth, had to load both pistols and show Canning how to cock one. Perhaps this was why Yarmouth, with an uncharacteristic twinge of conscience, suggested to Ellis that the protagonists, starting back to back, should each take six 'strides' away from the other in order to stand twelve paces apart, 'the longest distance for which there was any precedent'.

(Previous page) 'Killing no Murder or a New Ministerial way of settling the affairs of the Nation!' The 1809 duel between Castlereagh (shown on the left) and Canning as depicted by George Cruikshank within a day or two of the affair on London's Putney Heath.

Political cartoons were highly influential. They were reproduced in large numbers and displayed in the windows of print shops in major towns and cities (above)

According to advertising claims in that month's edition of *The British Duelling Pistol*, the finest of such firearms could guarantee accuracy over twenty paces 'in practised hands'. Although in contrast to his opponent a complete tyro, Canning almost had beginner's luck, his pistol ball passing through the button of the right lapel of Castlereagh's topcoat. His concentration disturbed by such a narrow escape, or so it was believed at the time, Castlereagh hesitated, fired… and unexpectedly missed. Despite protestations from both seconds, however, he was unwilling to let the matter rest there and the pistols were reloaded. This time Canning, who (as Ellis later reported) 'had not the slightest idea of taking aim', shot wildly and wide. Castlereagh, ignoring suggestions that he should point his pistol in the air, hit Canning on the outside of the left thigh.

His ball passed clean through the flesh without striking bone or muscle but came within a centimetre of a main artery, which would have proved fatal. Canning began to limp away but then stopped and asked Castlereagh, 'Are you sure we have done?' Lord Yarmouth said 'certainly'. Castlereagh did not reply, giving the impression that he would have preferred to fire again. In view of Canning's injury, this would certainly have been unprecedented. In 1836 the MP Grantley Buckley would exchange three rounds in a duel with a journalist but on that occasion none of the shots from either man struck their intended target.

George Canning (left) was a complete novice when it came to duelling whereas Viscount Castlereagh (right) was a crack shot who practised in his basement

The original cause of the quarrel lay in a fundamental disagreement between Canning and Castlereagh on the prosecution of the war. Castlereagh, looking for a way to frustrate Napoleon's commercial blockade and take control of the port of Antwerp, had backed an expedition to seize the Dutch island of Walcheren at the mouth of the River Scheldt. Despite meticulous planning, it proved to be a complete failure. Sickness ran through the British troops, who had to be withdrawn. Canning worked furiously behind the scenes in an effort to have Castlereagh held responsible and removed as war minister. On 9 September Castlereagh finally discovered the existence of the Cabinet plot. Even then, however, he was in a quandary about what to do and did not react immediately. He felt compelled to issue a challenge ten days later only because of an unexpected turn of events involving his wife.

Castlereagh, a handsome Irishman of fashion and elegance, if rather aloof and his conversation often marred by fractured syntax, was generally considered a fine catch. It was a surprise in April 1794 when at 25 he became betrothed to Amelia Hobart, daughter of the Earl of Buckinghamshire. Castlereagh had met her a year earlier on a visit to Bath. Emily, as she was known, seems to have indulged generously throughout her life in both food and drink. A rather sour acquaintance observed that 'Lady Emily is not a beauty; or if she is, it is a barn door one, without colour – very tall, fat and sweet countenanced and artless in appearance.'

Emily was also no great intellect but after her marriage to Castlereagh she threw herself enthusiastically into the relentless circuit of soirees, dances and balls that characterised London society.

Not everyone thought Emily Hobart's curves unattractive: one of Castlereagh's Irish contemporaries, John Prendergast, described her as 'A romping piece of flesh'

The height of fashion was Almack's, a Palladian mansion in King Street, a short distance from the Castlereaghs' own property in St James' Square. Back in 1765 Almack's three huge 'Assembly Rooms' had been lavishly refurbished and furnished by William Mackall. He used the profits from his first metropolitan venture, an up-market gambling club, the future Brook's, patronised by a set of young wealthy aristocrats. They called themselves the 'macaronis' (after an Italian dish they had tasted while on the Grand Tour) and bet foolish sums on unpromising hands of cards. Mackall, the former valet of the Duke of Hamilton, soon realised that Scotsmen were not popular among the London gentry. For his new venture he reversed the syllables of his name to disguise Almack's provenance.

What made Almack's so desirable was a mixture of snobbery and exclusivity. A ball was held on Wednesday evenings during the Season, marked by the end of fox-hunting as the ground hardened shortly before Christmas and the start of grouse shooting on August's 'Glorious Twelfth'. It was ruthlessly controlled by the 'ladies-patronesses'. They met in the club's Blue Chamber on Mondays and Thursdays to consider the latest applications for non-transferable annual vouchers affording access to Almack's, each priced at ten guineas. Many titled persons were reluctant to apply, for fear of refusal. As the English poet and wit Henry Luttrell wrote,

> 'All on that magic List depends;
> Fame, fortune, fashion, lovers, friends;
> 'Tis that which gratifies or vexes
> All ranks, all ages, and both sexes.
> If once to Almack's you belong,
> Like monarchs you can do no wrong;
> But banished thence on Wednesday night,
> By Jove, you can do nothing right.'

Unfortunately for Castlereagh, as one of Napoleon's biographers, the lawyer Philip Guedella remarked, 'How rarely statesman seem to realise the unintentional wisdom of annoying poets'. By bringing the quarrel between Cabinet colleagues out into the open, Almack's unwittingly pushed him over the edge. A few months before the duel, in the spring of 1809, Emily Castlereagh accepted an invitation to become a patroness, joining Clementina Drummond-Burrell, daughter of the Earl of Perth; Sarah Villiers, Countess of Jersey; and Amelia Lamb, Lady Cowper. At their meeting on 18 September Emily was surprised to learn of an application that ostensibly came from Canning to join Almack's. It was supported by a note from that supreme arbiter of fashion, Beau Brummell. If his cravat were not perfect at the first time of tying, it was cast into a pile of rejects, to the exasperation of his valet, who had probably the most thankless task in London. Tall, fair but with a prominent broken nose acquired in a fall while hunting – the fox got away – Brummell lived around the corner in Chesterfield Street, where he frequently entertained the Prince Regent for dinner.

For all that, Brummell's endorsement was not immediately persuasive. Emily considered Canning an upstart and social climber, whose mother, horror of all horrors, had been an actress. She knew that behind her back, Canning had made her the target of his caustic comments. Emily solemnly rejected the application but was eventually induced to change her mind by the vociferous protests of the younger patronesses. Canning, the only member of the Cabinet who was neither a peer nor the son of a peer, had little in common with any of them. The Countess of Jersey later admitted that they were simply curious to meet the principal conspirator in the plot against Castlereagh. It was already the subject of gossip among Almack's gentry but both he and his wife had been kept completely in the dark. Before long, Brummell was suspected of having mischievously handed over ten guineas for a voucher without Canning's knowledge. Not that he could afford it. Beau's bubble finally burst in 1816 when, unable to sustain the lifestyle of his social set from his meagre income, he fled to Calais to escape his creditors.

For Castlereagh, meanwhile, the implicit endorsement of Canning by his own wife must have been the last straw. It seemed Canning's machinations were known not only to his fellow conspirators in the Cabinet but also to half of London. This was especially galling because Castlereagh was the man who always prided himself in being one move ahead of everyone else. When he put down the Irish Rebellion of 1798, it was said that 'The backstairs to Castlereagh's sanctum were worn bare... and... so adroitly did he work on his puppets that they even informed upon each other, not knowing their fellow traitors'. The day after the meeting of the

Almack's Assembly Rooms, the brainchild of William Mackall, who reversed the syllables of his name to hide their Scottish provenance

Almack's staged a ball every Wednesday during the Season. Admission was ruthlessly controlled by the 'patronesses', led by Sarah Villiers, Countess of Jersey, shown here dancing, second on the left

patronesses, Castlereagh, humiliated and angry, sent a long, extraordinary letter to Canning, asserting that his rival's actions were 'at the expense of my Honour and Reputation' and demanding satisfaction. Canning had no choice but to play out his role as the intended victim in what the crusader against slavery, William Wilberforce, described as Castlereagh's 'cold-blooded measure of deliberate revenge'.

Eleven days after the sensational affair on Putney Heath, an army officer, Major Alexander Campbell, was hanged for shooting dead a fellow captain in a duel that took place in Ireland. This was a sobering reminder of the potential legal consequences whenever a fatality occurred. Despite Canning's rapid recovery from his flesh wound, the duel at a time of national crisis prompted widespread opprobrium. Both he and Castlereagh were forced to leave office. 'Lord Castlebrag', as the unpopular minister was known to many, came off the worse. All the front windows in the Castlereaghs' residence at No 18 St James' Square were broken and on one occasion Castlereagh himself, accosted by a mob and pelted with vegetables and excrement, had to take refuge inside a draper's shop in St Martin's Lane. Luckily for him the disturbance made such a noise that it attracted the attention of the diminutive George Townsend, the chief police officer of the Bow Street Runners. He arrived panting just in the nick of time, in his flaxen wig, holding on to his broad-brimmed hat, and together with several of his burly men took Castlereagh to safety.

As Castlereagh's father, a merchant, sat in the House of Lords only as the result of the Irish Act of Union in 1800, Canning's allies also vigorously questioned the Stewart family's antecedents. They delighted in repeating the scornful words of an Irish clergyman, the Reverend James Porter, later hanged for sedition. Porter knew the Stewarts before their elevation to the peerage and said, 'What a fine thing to see in one day, "Mr" changed into "My Lord", "Mrs" into "My Lady"; then comes the coronet painted on the coach, on the harness, on the dishes and plates, and the piss-pots.'

The Secretary at War was reliably reported to have practised for the duel with his beautiful pistols for hour after hour in the basement of his house. He almost deafened his servants with the noise of dangerous ricochets and left their quarters blighted with the smell of expended cartridges. In doing so he had broken the unwritten code, the exquisitely nuanced and peculiarly British concept of the 'amateur'.

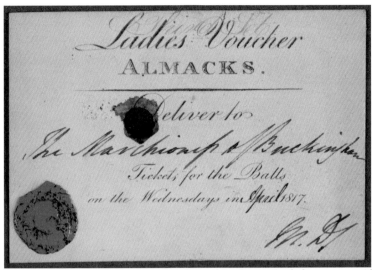

A rare surviving example of the coveted voucher that afforded access to Almack's

Beau Brummell put down Canning's name for Almack's without his knowledge, spending ten guineas he could ill afford, as in 1816 Beau had to flee to France to escape his creditors

It was all-pervasive among the upper classes and in many walks of political, military, religious and society life. Put simply, it was not done to be seen to be too good at anything, to be organised, to be, well, dare one say, professional. The adherence to amateurism allowed senior politicians to spend much of their day drinking claret – enormous quantities of claret. They saw no reason to be discreet. On the contrary, they chose such prominent places as the state-of-the-art Bay Window seat under construction by the front entrance of White's club, where they soon became visible but still impervious to the public at large.

Abroad, the duel rapidly became a cause celebre. Castlereagh was reckoned not so much an *arriviste* for his social elevation but rather a dilettante, with its connotation of seriousness that nonetheless fell just short of the social faux pas of being thought a professional. The concept of an amateur on the continent did not have quite the same cachet as in England. There was no word for it in Italian or German and in French, although spelled the same, it meant something different and somewhat derogatory. In 1768 the great philosopher, Jean-Jacques Rousseau, had defined 'amateur', initially in musical but later in broad sociological terms. According to him, two kinds of amateurs existed: those who were not professionals but who participated over eagerly with a modest and fallible degree of competence; and those who ineptly took part in activities they knew nothing about but pretended they did! The most significant consequence during the Napoleonic wars was that bungling, usually titled amateurs with influence at military headquarters in London's Horse Guards blighted the British Army. Fortunately for Britain, for years the English Channel and the Royal Navy kept Bonaparte and a huge, standing, experienced and undeniably professional French army at bay.

Chapter Two

Fiend of German Birth

FOR THE MOMENT Napoleon may have been the master of Europe but like other rulers in other courts he remained conveniently isolated from the harsh realities of everyday life. During the winter of 1808 to 1809, nearly 600,000 of Europe's lowlier citizens died of cold, disease or starvation. That autumn Emperor proceeded obliviously on a quasi-royal progress and on 2 October 1808 met the great German author Johann Wolfgang von Goethe over breakfast during the Congress of Erfurt. Goethe was flattered to learn that Napoleon regarded his novel *The Sorrows of Young Werther* as a literary masterpiece. Completed in less than three months early in 1774, the work, a tragic love triangle, had turned the 24-year-old Goethe from a struggling writer into an international celebrity almost overnight. Napoleon told Goethe he had taken the French translation with him on his Egyptian campaign and read it among the Pyramids, in all no fewer than seven times. To prove this he quoted extensive passages from memory, including one where Werther dances with his true love, Lotte, at a ball:

'When the waltz commenced… never have I moved so lightly. I was no longer a human being. To hold in my arms the most adorable creature in the world and to fly around with her like the wind, so that everything around us fades into nothing…'

The waltz had reached such heady heights of imperial approval from humble beginnings. It had its origins as a variation of the Volta, a French creation from the time of the troubadours and a favourite of Elizabeth I. So vigorous was the Volta, ladies of the English Court often had to excuse themselves to change their under-garments during the course of an evening's entertainment.

Napoleon demonstrates to Goethe how he was captivated by his description of a waltz, reading it time and time again under the shadow of the Pyramids

The leaping movement of the Volta reached its climax in the ländler, a German peasant dance. The height that a woman's skirt reached as she leapt upwards was thought to determine the height that the annual corn crop would grow: the perfect excuse for the man to toss his partner in the air as high as possible. The preceding spinning movement of the dancers was known as *'walzen'*, to 'revolve' or 'turn'. By the mid-18th century the use of the word as a verb had developed to describe the dance itself. The waltz first appeared in a musical comedy, performed in 1750 by the Viennese clown Gottfried Prehauser, where he encourages the audience to join in:

> *'Balden walzen umadum*
> *Mit heirassa drum'*
> *('Turn about waltzing*
> *And cheer as you turn')*

As enthusiasm for the waltz gathered momentum, even the most illustrious composers had to go with the flow to put bread on the table. In 1766 Joseph Haydn produced his *Mouvement de Waltze*, the first known waltz intended for a piano, influenced he confessed by competition 'to innovate'. Over the next decade, the waltz became almost unstoppable. Austria was in the vanguard, led by the Austrian Emperor, Joseph II, brother of Marie Antoinette. Joseph hated the Hofburg Palace in Vienna, where he was surrounded by nobles and officials who secretly sneered at him as a parvenu from Lorraine. He favoured the emancipation of his peasants and in 1773, much to the indignation of his nobility, decided to open the palace ballrooms to the common man. This started the tradition of public balls in Vienna and at the same time introduced the upper crust to that favourite dance of the commoner, the waltz. The languass, a frenzied two-step waltz in which the female partner is frequently thrown high in the air, became so popular at the Hofburg that a city ordinance was introduced to regulate it. Palace officials patrolled the ballrooms to prevent ladies' undergarments from being exposed.

The novelist Sophie von La Roche jilted her Swiss fiancée in favour of a German nobleman born the wrong side of the blanket to a dancer. In such circumstances she might have been expected to support the waltz but instead became one of its most dogged opponents. Her 1771 *Story of Fraulein von Sternheim*, when the heroine is experiencing the waltz at a ball for the first time, left no doubt about Sophie's negative view of predatory dancing partners:

'…but when he put his arm around her, pressed to her breast, cavorted with her in the shameless whirling-dance of the Germans and engaged in a familiarity that broke all the bounds of good breeding - then silent misery turned into burning rage.'

Visiting London to promote the English translation, Sophie was mortified to discover that a work she intended to be morally instructive of young women had instead heightened their passions. It left them desperate to try the wicked dance for themselves.

In 1786 the Spanish composer, Vicenz Martin y Soler, included a waltz in the second act of his opera, *Una Cosa Rara*, danced by the four principals. This was marked andante con moto, or 'at a walking pace with

Sophie von La Roche intended her story about the 'shameless whirling-dance' of the Germans to be morally instructive of young women but instead it made them eager to try the wicked waltz for themselves

Gottfried or Godefridus Prehauser, comedian, clown and comic genius.
His impromptu sketches encouraged audience participation… and they began to waltz

*The ländler was the forerunner of the waltz, a peasant dance in which the
higher a woman was lifted off the ground, the higher their corn would grow –
or so men claimed*

motion', scarcely ground-breaking stuff. Nonetheless it received rapturous
applause in Vienna. The production run was extended for the whole season
at the expense of Wolfgang Amadeus Mozart, whose own opera, *Figaro*,
was abandoned. Mozart was furious and to make certain it did not happen
to him again, included a waltz in *Don Giovanni*, launched the following
year. Mozart both danced and played at the Hofburg, whose balls became
the Viennese way of celebrating the winter season known as carnival.
He wrote the waltz music for the 1791 carnival ball, some of whose original
scores survive. Mozart increased its speed by composing orchestral dances
based on the ländler in triple time. By 1797, according to the contemporary
fashion *Journal des Luxas und der Moden*, the swift turns and tempo of

The waltz as observed in Bavaria: 'The hand holding the dress lay hard against the breasts, pressing lasciviously at every movement'

the Viennese waltz such as the *Geschwindwalzer*, and the *Galloppwalzer* 'surpassed everything in headlong speed'. Said the *Journal*, 'waltzes and nothing but waltzes are now so much the fashion that at dances nothing else is looked at'.

The faster the waltz, the more the prospect of it shocked London society. Haydn gave a celebrated recital including his waltz composition in front of an invited audience in a house on Hanover Square, but still the patronesses of Almack's refused point blank to allow such music near their dance floor. They received a note of support through diplomatic channels from the queen consort of Prussia, Frederika Louisa of Hesse-Darmstadt. Frederika had been so shocked by the waltz when it was introduced at a court ball in the spring of 1794 by her husband Frederick William II - a serial adulterer widely known in diplomatic circles as *der dicke Lüderjahn* ('the fat scallywag') - that she banned it altogether.

Scandalous tales came back to Britain from the continent. In 1798 one traveller, Ernst Moritz Arndt, observed a waltz in a Bavarian village near Erlangen. 'The dancers held up the dresses of their partners very high so that they should not trail and be stepped on,' he wrote. However after this seemingly innocent beginning, the dancers used the dress as a shroud, wrapping themselves 'under one covering, as close together as possible…and thus protected, the turning went on in the most indecent positions.' Arndt did not spare himself or his intended audience the more prurient detail. 'The hand holding the dress lay hard against the breasts, pressing lasciviously at every movement', he said, 'and the girls, meanwhile, looked half mad and ready to swoon.' Arndt also observed that as the couples 'waltzed around on the darker side of the room, their embraces and kisses grew still bolder'.

What truly challenged the puritannical climate at Almack's, however, was the arrival in London during the spring of 1812 of Baron Philipp Roger Franz Freiherr von Neumann, initially on extended leave between diplomatic postings. Baron Neumann was born in Vienna and educated in Brussels. He was fluent in English, having improved his knowledge of the language, it was maliciously alleged, between the silk Parisian sheets of the wife of a British plenipontentary.

Neumann was the supreme ladies' man, whom Prince Paul Esterházy III, the Austrian ambassador to the Court of St James, said 'held the commanding position in all the world' when it came to women. Esterhazy's admiration might have been less fervent if he had known that Neumann was bedding his wife, Her Serene Highness Maria Theresia. She was a hereditary princess of Thurn and Taxis, two pocket German states in the Holy Roman Empire that held a lucrative monopoly to operate the imperial postal service. The niece of Queen Charlotte, George III's wife, Maria Theresia had impeccable connections. Although still only 18, she was invited to become one of Almack's patronesses. Pretty, plump and a stickler for protocol, she wore down opposition to the waltz by a mixture of charm and cunning. Neumann, appointed a temporary secretary at the Austrian embassy in London's Chandos Square, organised a ball at Almack's on her behalf with a card containing no fewer than five waltzes.

The German princess Maria Theresia became an Almack's patroness. Pretty, plump and a stickler for protocol, she wore down opposition to the waltz by a mixture of charm and cunning

By the standards of the time, this unparalleled opportunity for young men to touch women who were almost complete strangers, and close to their forbidden parts, was a heady, erotic experience. It horrified Almack's more conservative patrons. One, firmly declining to whirl around the salons, observed 'Baron de Neumann perpetually turning with the Princess Esterhazy....Requiring a close-up face to face position, with the

(Previous page) Lord Byron and Lady Caroline Lamb had a notorious turbulent affair. Byron visited ballrooms despite his club foot so Lady Caroline did not dance but sat out even her favourite waltzes. The relationship did not last

gentleman's arm round the lady's waist.' She described the waltz as 'this fiend of German birth... equally destitute of grace, delicacy and propriety... a disgusting practice'. In private, the Baron responded that an English dance in contrast was *'charakterloses getrippel, etwas pferdetrottmaessiges'* ('characterless tripping, a bit like a horse trotting').

Between March and August 1812 the most glittering star of Regency London, Lord Byron, had a turbulent affair with Lady Caroline Ponsonby Lamb, the wife of Viscount William Lamb, later Lord Melbourne, Queen Victoria's first prime minister. Lady Caroline loved to waltz but Byron's club foot rendered him unable to dance, so instead she loyally sat with him gazing wistfully at the ballroom floor. On 5 July 1813, just after Byron had refused to revive the relationship, both were invited by Katherine Sophia, Lady Heathcote, to a waltzing party at her London mansion. The vengeful Lady Caroline came up to Byron and said, 'I conclude I may waltz again now'. Byron replied, casting a slur on her morality, '... with everyone in turn: I have been admiring your dexterity.' Lady Caroline broke a glass and half-heartedly attempted to slash her wrists but as Byron continued to taunt her, fled from the scene.

Shortly afterwards Byron devoted a whole poem to *The Waltz* that pandered to the worst prejudices of mothers protective of their daughters:

> *'From where the garb just leaves the bosom free,*
> *That spot where hearts were once supposed to be,*
> *Round all the confines of the yielded waist,*
> *The stranger's hand may wander undisplaced.*
> *The breast thus publicly resign'd to man*
> *In private may resist him — if it can.'*

Byron's poem was published anonymously, apparently prompted by a letter in a newspaper from a Midland Member of Parliament. He recounted that he had left a ballroom because of a call of nature and returned to find his wife waltzing 'with her arms half round the loins of a huge hussar-looking gentleman I never set eyes on before'.

However when Byron was compelled to admit his authorship, he sounded an entirely different note. He of all people was not in a position to take a high moral tone. The poet had embarked on affairs with both men and women and an incestuous relationship with his own half-sister, Augusta Leigh. The hero of the Romantic Movement, with its emphasis on impromptu music and spontaneity, disingenuously pretended his purpose all along had been to recognise the instant and widespread appeal of the waltz in dance halls across England. Byron's threadbare excuse rested on his poem's final stanza, personifying the waltz as a beautiful woman:

'To one and all the lovely stranger came,
And every ball-room echoes with her name.'

Not quite every ballroom. Although in London round one had gone to Princess Esterhazy, the Countess of Jersey remained determined not to allow the waltz at Almack's on a regular basis. In modern terms, Sarah Villiers was a millionairess, with immense influence. After her future mother had eloped to Gretna Green to marry the Earl of Westmorland against the wishes of her outraged parents, in due course Sarah became the direct beneficiary of their will, with an income from Child's Bank of £60,000 a year, a huge fortune at the time. Regarding herself as *primus inter pares*– the other patronesses referred to her as "Queen Sarah" because of her airs and graces – she refused admission tickets to Almack's to any aspiring male applicant who had expressed the slightest enthusiasm for the waltz. One captain in the 3rd brigade of the Grenadier Guards, furious at his very public and abrupt rejection, attempted to challenge her husband, George Villiers, 5th Earl of Jersey, to a duel. Lord Jersey replied saying that 'if all the persons who did not receive tickets from my wife were to call me to account for want of courtesy on her part, then I would be a constant target for young officers, and must decline the honour'.

He had no illusions about his wife's fidelity. Sarah was said to have had too many affairs to keep count. When a close friend asked Lord Jersey why he had never called out one of her lovers, if only to preserve his family's reputation, the earl dryly replied this would set such a precedent that he would end up fighting a duel with every gentleman in London. Lord Jersey was nothing if not long-suffering because he also had to

Sarah Villiers, Countess of Jersey (above) and her mother-in-law Frances Villiers,
Lady Jersey (left) vied for the title of most promiscuous member of the British
aristocracy. Sarah had too many affairs to keep count; half of Frances's ten children
came from adulterous liaisons

contend with the equally shameless conduct of his mother, distinguished from the Countess as *Lady* Jersey. Frances Villiers gave birth to at least ten children between 1771 and 1788, but the most reliable estimates of the number actually fathered by her husband George vary between five and six. Frances always aimed high: her lovers included Frederick Howard, 5th Earl of Carlisle and William Cavendish, 5th Duke of Devonshire. It mattered not one jot to Frances that her supposed best friend was Cavendish's wife, the Duchess of Devonshire, Georgiana. In 1782 she was propositioned at a ball by the 25-year-old Prince of Wales but turned him down because he was 'too inexperienced, too notorious, too much in debt'. 'Prinny' had to wait almost ten years for his turn, when Frances was already a grandmother. Their liaison lasted six years and the prince installed Frances and her compliant husband in a house next door to his official residence in Carlton House.

Chapter Three

Stand and Deliver

IN THE EPIC double standards and hypocrisy of the time, despite her deeply embarrassing mother-in-law, the Countess of Jersey could sustain her position among the patronesses because scarcely any of them – poor plump Emily apart – was in a position to cast the first stone. Sarah lived in fear however that if the biggest skeleton in the family closet came to light, she would become both a social pariah and a laughing stock. Incredible though it may seem, Sarah's grandfather-in-law, the Right Reverend Philip Twysden, who died violently aged 38, three months before her birth, was both an Anglican bishop and a highwayman.

Twysden, born in Kent, the third son of Sir William Twysden, 5th Baronet, gained an M.A. at University College Oxford and was subsequently awarded the honorary degree of Doctorate of Civil Law. His first ecclesiastical posting was as Rector of Ealing and later he was appointed Lord Bishop of Raphoe in County Donegal in the north of Ireland. It would be hard to find a more respectable background but his Irish living brought in very little and Twysden had spent his way through his small share of the family fortune. In order to stave off bankruptcy, the bishop by day became a highwayman by night. His modus operandi seems to have been to attend the sick and dying who possessed the means to summon an affluent doctor, to discover the physician's likely route onwards to his next patient, and secretly to unload his pistols, leaving him unarmed and powerless when Twysden, in disguise, later asked him to stand and deliver.

His preferred location for each hold-up was known as Hounslow Heath, conveniently close to the coaching junction of Hounslow, where passengers changed coaches either to travel north or into London. On the present site of London Airport, in the early 18th century Hounslow Heath, still heavily wooded, was one of the most dangerous places in Britain. The Bath Road, carrying courtiers to Windsor and the gentry to the West Country, ran right across it. Apart from a few menacing taverns, where only the likes of Dick Turpin would feel safe, it was completely deserted and ideal for an ambush.

Hounslow Heath was one of the most dangerous places in Britain for coach passengers in the 19th century. Although the corpses of convicted highwaymen hanged at Tyburn Tree were strung up on the heath as a deterrent, hold-ups still regularly took place

The stately home of Osterley Park to where the unmasked highwayman-bishop, the Reverend Twysden (insert, right), was taken suffering from a terminal bullet wound to the stomach

Twysden used an alias, 'Dumas', when dealing with jewel fences, suggesting that highway robbery was for him a regular source of income. What made 1 November 1752 different was that the patient to whom Twysden administered the last rites stayed conscious long enough to warn the doctor that his pistols had been tampered with. Unknown to Twysden, when later that evening he stopped the doctor's coach, his victim was an armed and alert man who had reloaded his pistols. He promptly shot the masked highwayman in the stomach. Discovering he was none other than the bishop, the doctor, horrified by the looming scandal, put the dying man in his coach and drove furiously back to Osterley Park. This grand home on the north-east perimeter of the heath was owned by the banking family from where Sarah, Countess of Jersey would derive her fortune. Shortly afterward, at the urgent behest of his reluctant hosts, he wrote a death certificate describing the cause as 'inflammation of the bowels'. With the Establishment looking after its own, Twysden's body was transferred by hearse to his house in Jermyn Street. The family placed an announcement in the *London Evening News* to the effect that the bishop had died of natural causes. He was finally laid to rest, conspicuously bereft of a headstone, in East Peckham Church. The *Gentleman's Magazine* got wind of what had really happened but could only hint at the potential scandal. The best informed were Twysden's Irish parishioners, one of whom was a close relative of the third parlour maid at Osterley Park.

The Countess of Jersey, whom Twysden also never lived to see, gave both her favours and a free annual pass for Almack's to a mere ensign in the Welsh Grenadier Guards, Rees Howell Gronow. A handsome dandy who regularly neglected his guard duties at St James' Palace to attend the club, Gronow's public gratitude was overflowing, as to him, Almack's was 'the seventh heaven of the fashionable world.' Sarah might have been less generous had she known what Gronow privately thought of her: 'a theatrical tragedy queen, who simply made herself look ridiculous, being inconceivably rude and ill-bred in her manner'. Gronow had no illusions about the scruples of any of the committee. 'Many diplomatic arts, and much finesse, and a host of intrigues', he reported, 'were set in motion to get an invitation to Almack's… the female government… was a pure despotism and… like every other despotism, it was not innocent of abuses'.

The Countess of Jersey realised that she needed a high-born counterweight to Princess Esterhazy among the patronesses. She lighted upon the wife of a newly arrived Russian diplomat and later ambassador, Count Christopher von Lieven. The elegant, haughty Daria (anglicised as Dorothea) Christoforovna Benkendorff was a member of the Russian Baltic nobility from Riga, where her father had been military governor. Dorothea's arranged marriage at sixteen to Count von Lieven was far from being a love match, leaving her to find solace elsewhere. Countess, later Princess, von Lieven took to diplomatic adultery like a duck to water, devoting herself tirelessly to the interests of Russia, with access to many of its political secrets. Her lovers changed with each British Cabinet reshuffle and she bedded almost every major personage on the European stage, including the Austrian Chancellor, Count Clemens von Metternich, and George IV.

Rees Gronow of the Grenadier Guards, a Welsh dandy, slept with the Countess of Jersey but thought her 'inconceivably rude and ill-bred'

Countess von Lieven took to diplomatic adultery like a duck to water. Her lovers changed with each British Cabinet reshuffle

Dorothea's charisma and intelligence made her more than a match for Princess Esterhazy, whom she dismissed as 'small, round, black, animated and spiteful'. They often had words – extremely rude words for those familiar with Russian - across the red tablecloth at Almack's that marked the patronesses' meetings. However, much to the Countess of Jersey's surprise and indignation, Dorothea saw the way society winds were blowing. Far from objecting to the waltz, she actively supported it. Two years later she would play her trump card. Dorothea encouraged Tsar Alexander I, on an official visit, to disregard those parts of the programme that did not appeal to him.. Alexander had an increasingly fractious relationship with the Prince Regent, arriving at points on the agreed itinerary either hours before or hours after him and constantly embarrassing the British government. He refused the Prince's invitation to stay at St James' Palace and instead took a suite just down the street from Almack's at the Pulteney Hotel in Piccadilly. A day or two later the Tsar decided he wanted to waltz at Almack's. He did so wearing 'his tight uniform and numerous decorations', even though Almack's was not on the itinerary at all and the orchestra had no sheet music for a waltz in their evening repertoire. After such a prodigious royal seal of approval, even 'Queen Sarah' bowed to the inevitable and in future allowed the waltz to be included regularly on the programme.

Much to the Countess of Jersey's chagrin, Dorothea also proved to be an exceptionally accomplished dancer. She first took the floor for the waltz with Castlereagh's successor at the war ministry, John Henry Temple, Viscount Palmerston. He purchased a new pair of pumps for the occasion and had been practising its steps with his sister Fanny at her afternoon 'dancing parties'. Dorothea's motives for her choice of partner were extremely suspect, to say the least. Palmerston's mistress was widely known to be her co-patroness, Amelia, Countess Cowper, Lady Caroline Lamb's sister-in-law.

Amelia was the most popular member of the Lamb family, leading lights among the Whigs. However her mother, Elizabeth Milbanke, showed such startling promiscuity that Elizabeth's husband Peniston Lamb, Viscount Melbourne, was thought unlikely to be the father and Amelia's true parentage remained 'shrouded in mystery'. This may help to explain why as a dazzling beauty of eighteen, she was married off to a man nine years her senior whom, despite his title, no rational parents could possibly have found an attractive match. Her husband, Peter Clavering-Cowper, the 5th Earl Cowper, was a man of singular mental dullness and slowness of speech. Guests who dozed off at his dinner table could awake several minutes later not having missed a single word. As the earl disliked society and politics almost as much as the enthusiastic participants in each disliked him, Amelia had free rein to make her mark in both. Warm-hearted and generous,

Amelia Lamb, Countess Cowper, another of Almack's patronesses, was considered warm-hearted and generous but the concept of time-keeping completely passed her by

Viscount Palmerston, Amelia's lover, used her to try out potential diplomatic initiatives on unsuspecting foreigners on Almack's dance floor

Pub.^d May 18th 1813 by
H. Humphrey, St James's Street

LONGITUDE & LATIT

G. Cruikshank fec^t

(previous page) The improbable but almost certainly platonic partnership of two Russians, the obese Prince Kozlowsky and the tall, slim Countess von Lieven. They danced together at Almack's and inspired a George Cruikshank cartoon entitled 'The Longitude and Latitude of St Petersburg'

she granted an interview to and captivated a correspondent of the *London Times*, who described her in print as 'grace put in action, [whose] softness was as seductive as her joyousness'. Like many titled ladies occasionally seen with their husbands in the corridors of the House of Lords, however, the concept of time-keeping completely passed her by. Her most patient lover, Carlo Andrea Pozzo di Borgo, later Russian ambassador in London, found the capital a welcome haven from his fellow Corsican, Napoleon, until he was recalled in 1812.

Viscount Palmerston proved an ideal replacement for Borgo in her bed, not least because his lateness at any rendezvous made Amelia seem positively punctual. As guest tickets at Almack's were eagerly snapped up by foreign ambassadors, Palmerston would encourage his mistress casually to speculate inside the club on a seemingly hypothetical diplomatic initiative, right in front of a chosen target, thereby advising him of their reaction before it became official government policy. Indispensable though Amelia became to him, Palmerston, known for good reason as 'Cupid' by his cronies, nonetheless had a wandering eye. This turned his highly prominent dance partnership with Dorothea into an anxious evening for her. The increasingly congested dance floor made it easy for the couple, as if by common consent, to describe an infinite number of increasingly tight and intimate circles. But as it turned out, Amelia need not have worried, for the moment at least, that she would lose her lover's affections. Dorothea tried to pay Palmerston a compliment by telling him: 'if I were not Russian, I should like to have been English.' Palmerston ungallantly replied in sexist fashion: 'If I were not English, I should like to have been an Englishman.'

After this temporary rebuff, Dorothea rejected other aspiring but less desirable English partners in favour of a Russian diplomat of her own, one who rivalled the Prince Regent in the size of his girth. Prince Peter Borisovich Kozlowsky, passing through London on the way to represent his country in Sardinia, proved to be a dazzling wit and surprisingly fleet of foot. The improbable discrepancy in Almack's ballroom between the tall, slim Countess von Lieven and the short, prodigiously obese Prince Kozlowsky was a gift for a cartoonist like George Cruikshank, who entitled his work *The Longitude and Latitude of St Petersburg.*

Although not something he was keen to mention in London, during a rare cessation of hostilities between the great powers Kozlowsky had received the legion d'honneur from Napoleon himself, for helping a group of French officers to escape from English captivity. Kozlowsky claimed to have encouraged the Emperor to learn the waltz in order to impress his second wife, the Austrian archduchess, 18-year-old Marie Louise. The marriage began happily enough in April 1810 when, after the couple's first night together, the 40-year-old Napoleon boasted of his sexual skills to one of his generals: 'She liked it so much that she asked me to do it again'. On 1 July Napoleon intended to demonstrate to his wife his progress in learning the waltz during a celebratory ball at the Austrian embassy in Paris but the first such dance of the evening proved to be the last. A candelabra left too close to a flimsy curtain set it alight. The entire building in the rue de Mont Blanc rapidly burned to the ground. The unworldly Marie Louise escaped only when Napoleon seized her by the hand himself and led his new bride to safety. Many were not so fortunate. The fatal casualties included the sister-in-law of Karl Philipp, Prince von Schwarzenberg, Austria's flamboyant cavalry commander.

The shy, timid archduchess Marie Louise of Austria became Napoleon's second wife. During their brief courtship he learned the waltz to please her.

Napoleon planned to demonstrate his prowess in a ball at the Austrian embassy in Paris but fire broke out and the Emperor had to lead Marie Louise to safety

Louise Aglaé Auguié, the wife of Marshal Michel Ney, encouraged a much more athletic French version of the waltz

Marshal Ney, having changed sides to support Napoleon's return to power, had four horses shot from under him at Waterloo but was declared a traitor by the Bourbons

Bonaparte's own spectacular cavalry commander, although by no means his ablest tactician, was Michel Ney, from Alsace, bilingual in French and German. Napoleon regarded him as 'the bravest of the brave' and indulged him tremendously, albeit at others' expense. The Empress Josephine found Ney a wife, Louise Aglaé Auguié, whose mother had been a lady-in-waiting to the ill-fated Marie Antoinette. The couple married in August 1802 and in 1805 Ney acquired, at a fraction of its true value, the Parisian hôtel de Saisseval, overlooking the Seine. A word from the Emperor here, a word there, and manufacturers throughout Europe proved eager to help furnish the vast property, without so much as presenting a bill. The mansion played host to a series of magnificent entertainments. Madame Ney is credited with encouraging an athletic French version of the waltz, performed on the ball of the foot. It consisted of three different movements joined together by pirouettes, ever increasing in speed, and

(opposite) Francisco Goya brilliantly captured the cares of command in his candid portrait of the Duke of Wellington during the Peninsular War, shortly after his entry into Madrid in 1812

culminating in springs and leaps. The hôtel de Saisseval's fortunes declined after the end of the First Empire and it would be demolished in 1866.

The man who would prove Napoleon's nemesis, Arthur Wellesley, the future Duke of Wellington, was born in Dublin in 1769. His real name was Wesley but his family changed it, thinking Wellesley sounded grander. One of Wesley's ancestors was an Anne Wellesley, back in the 16th century. Despite his military successes in India, when he returned to London in 1805, few people had heard of him. On 12 September Wellesley found himself waiting in Castlereagh's anti-room at the Colonial Office in Downing Street with none other than Lord Nelson, who made an excuse to go outside and ask an equerry who he was. Thanks to the minister's tardiness, the two great heroes then talked for an hour, on the eve of Nelson's return to the fleet, culminating in his death at the battle of Trafalgar. Wellesley was given command of Britain's troops in Portugal, one of Castlereagh's last decisions as Minister at War. It easily might never have been. In June 1808 he was about to sail from Ireland to South America with a 9,000 strong expeditionary force to assist rebels in the Spanish colonies when a much more promising rebellion against French rule flared up in Spain itself, and he was nearly shipwrecked on the way to Lisbon; but destiny called.

Chapter Four

The Congress Dances

IN 1812 CASTLEREAGH, fully vindicated in his support for Wellesley, who had forced the French out of Portugal and was outwitting them in Spain, returned to the Cabinet as Foreign Secretary. The political dynamic was shifting in Britain's favour. The European powers soon became emboldened by Napoleon's disastrous retreat from Moscow but they lacked any clear plan to end the war. Castlereagh picked his way delicately through a quagmire of vested interests, becoming probably the first British Foreign Secretary to travel abroad on diplomatic missions on a regular basis. From the start it was not a comfortable experience. Accompanied by Emily, who refused to be left behind, he left London on Boxing Day 1813 in a thick fog. Castlereagh spent three nights becalmed in a British frigate off Harwich and was then battered by a snowstorm in the North Sea for another three days before landing safely in Holland. After a further gruelling week on the road in a coach and four, confronted with huge potholes and menaced by 'deserters and malcontents', Castlereagh arrived in Basle. He was due to hold talks with representatives from Austria, Prussia and Russia, already engaged in 'carving up Europe like a piece of cheese'. The Prussian ambassador to Vienna, Wilhelm von Humboldt, sent to greet Castlereagh, found him exhausted but nonetheless immaculately dressed in a blue coat with gold braid, red waistcoat and breeches. Wilhelm afterwards confessed to his wife that he could not help thinking the British Foreign Secretary resembled a flunkey at a ball.

And balls there were, to celebrate the liberation of German territories from French rule when the big three Continental allies entered Frankfurt early in November 1813. Titled ladies flocked to the first, as guests of the Russian Czar, Alexander I. Unfortunately the edicts of Queen Frederika banning the waltz had left most of the German aristocracy entirely ignorant of its steps and floundering

*Austrian Emperor Francis I returns to Vienna to cheers from his subjects
following the Peace of Paris in June 1814*

on the rather uneven dance floor. Collision after collision occurred and eventually resulted in a huge pile-up, with the dancers all collapsing in a heap. For one young woman in particular, and the male bystanders, it proved a memorable moment. The most inaccessible undergarment of the day consisted of a pair of drawers, literally two separate pieces of linen drawn up to the waist but open between the legs. 'All her secrets were revealed to everyone', said Metternich in a gleeful note dispatched to amuse his precocious daughter, Maria Leopoldina.

France and Napoleon continued their rear-guard action, bloody skirmishes alternating with failed diplomacy. Castlereagh's endless patience, adroit manoeuvring and combination of personal charm and tenacity, kept armies in the field and diplomats at the negotiating table. With Wellington already fighting his way through France, in April 1814 Bonaparte was finally dethroned, although presciently advising the newly restored Bourbons to change nothing but the sheets. The great European powers could not agree on what to do with their embarrassing prisoner. After much wrangling they decided, with no doubt an intentional touch of cruel irony, that the legend who had ruled over 70 million Europeans could be Emperor of... Elba, a tiny Mediterranean island between Corsica and the west coast of Italy, with just 12,000 inhabitants.

Negotiations to determine the future shape of post-Napoleonic Europe now began in earnest. A European peace conference was arranged, for which nearly 100,000 foreigners descended on Vienna in the autumn of 1814. They included the heads of five great reigning dynasties, members of 216 noble families, 700 diplomats and a retinue of courtiers, family members, domestic servants, secretariats and assorted camp followers.

En route to the Congress, Castlereagh reached Paris at dusk on 24 August. In another war half a world away, that same night British troops would eat the American president's dinner and set fire to the White House. Castlereagh spent three days with the newly elevated Duke of Wellington. His military successes against the revolutionary French had made him the ideal choice from the perspective of the Bourbons to be the first peacetime ambassador to France. The British delegation then set out for Vienna. They quickly rejected as too small the accommodation set aside for them by the Austrians at No 1 in the narrow street called Milchgasse, the very house in which Mozart had lived as a lodger in his teens and dashed off his first opera. Instead, they rented a suite of 22 rooms conveniently close to Metternich's official residence in the Ballhausplatz. Castlereagh and his wife took over the top floor, with its large receiving hall, where each Tuesday Emily held musical evenings. Her priority, however, was to bring her husband up to speed on the waltz, which had passed him by in his years of political exile. He was not a natural dancer but gangly and extremely ungainly.

Despite his protests, his wife hired a dancing instructor, who four times a week put the Foreign Secretary through his paces like some rebellious thoroughbred. Whenever Emily, unable to resist Vienna's haberdashery shops, failed to appear, depriving him of his partner, Castlereagh was made to practise holding a heavy wooden chair.

The Foreign Secretary's two maids had been hired directly by his staff to try to prevent the contents of the diplomatic wastepaper basket ending up in the hands of Baron Franz von Hager von Allentsteig, the Austrian Chief of Police, who ran a spurious domestic agency for just such a purpose. They were heard to remark sardonically to each other that if anything the shape and weight of the chair under-represented the demanding measurements of Castlereagh's wife. Emily's fashion sense made no sense at all. She purchased dresses in Vienna split to her ample thighs and pushing up her enormous bosom so that any waltzing partner had only to drop his eyes to see her nipples. Prince von Schwarzenberg was particularly indiscreet. 'She is very fat,' he told his allies, 'and dresses so young, so tight, so naked'. Castlereagh never ventured to query Emily's taste but started to rise at dawn so he could finish his papers and take time off in the afternoons to accompany his wife to the shops. He made sure that however many extravagant ball gowns she tried on, hardly any was actually purchased. A French courtesan, also newly arrived in Vienna from Paris but in her case for its easy pickings, watched the couple take their customary leave of one frustrated haberdashers. 'England is famous for its beautiful women', she announced to the customers with looser purse strings, 'but when they are ugly, *mon dieu* are they ugly!"

Every dress designer in Vienna worked day and night to finish their creations during the week preceding the official opening of the Congress on 2 October. It was celebrated by a great masked ball at the Hofburg Palace, spread across two ballrooms and the indoor riding school, linked together by avenues of orange trees in red and gold tubs. At 10 p.m. the entire Austrian Court descended magnificent twin staircases to the ground level of the riding school, which had been boarded over and ringed with seating for guests to watch the dancing. Rows of elaborate chandeliers decorated the school and throughout the evening 500 servants with long tapers were deployed to light, replace and re-light more than 15,000 candles, their shimmering effect reflected and magnified in huge mirrors covering every window.

The indiscriminate list of invitations, numbering just under 10,000, inevitably included a number of ladies who were heavily pregnant. As nothing would persuade them to stay at home, or to stay off the dance floor, six rooms at the Hofburg were designated as birthing chambers, 'with every convenience for their accouchement, should they unfortunately be required'.

The Czar led the opening waltz with Maria Ludovica, the Empress of Austria. Maria, who suffered from consumption, collapsed during the festivities and had to be carried by her ladies in waiting to her bedroom. She had gamely held out until midnight, when female guests were allowed to remove their masks and reveal their identities. By then these disguises had enabled many gate crashers to join the official guests by bribing the doormen checking invitations. Nearly all the guests, legitimate or otherwise, were on the lookout for souvenirs. Of 10,000 silver spoons laid out for supper, 3,000 were stolen. Maria's husband, Emperor Francis I, complained to her bitterly: 'If this goes on I shall abdicate. I can't stand this life much longer.'

Empress Maria Ludovica of Austria collapsed during the opening ball at the Hofburg Palace and had to be carried off the dance floor. She suffered from consumption and died two years later

The wags in Vienna had this to say about the principal monarchs at the Congress:

The Emperor of Russia makes love for everyone.
The King of Prussia thinks for everyone.
The Emperor of Austria (left) pays for everyone.

But carry on he did: holding a lavish ball every week until the end of the Congress. Francis I was compelled to raise taxes by almost 50 per cent to avoid Austria going bankrupt. He avoided riots in Vienna only by ordering the vast quantities of uneaten food to be laid out after the balls on trestle tables outside his palace, for the benefit of his disgruntled citizens.

The Czar remained at the official opening until 4 a.m., when the weary musicians rebelled and refused to strike up another tune. An exceptionally vain man, Alexander was rumoured to rub his face every morning with a chip from a block of ice to tighten the skin. However, like other less illustrious monarchs and their families, he would quickly find that the aura of hereditary rule was rapidly dispelled by regular contact with ordinary people at a succession of balls. The Swiss delegate Edmond Pictet said that royalty frantically waltzing away like university students was a 'curious spectacle…one false step, and you risk treading on the toe of an Emperor'. Or indeed worse. Accustomed to blind obedience and subservience in Russia, Alexander had a penchant for the ladies. He was furious when a 21-year-old beauty, Anna Eynard-Lullin, daughter of one Swiss banker and the wife of another, politely declined his spontaneous invitation to waltz. The Czar impetuously tore up her dance card; she called him an oaf. 'Alexander was thunderstruck that anyone should have the impudence to tell him with frankness what he was', she wrote in her diary. It was not, however, the Czar's most crushing rejection. At Count Palffly's ball, seeing Countess Julianna Szechenyi deserted by her spouse for another lady as the music stopped, he thought it an opportune moment to approach *la beauté coquette*. 'Your husband seems to have left you', was his opening sally, 'It would give me enormous pleasure to occupy his place'. The Countess retorted: 'Does Your Majesty mistake me for a Polish province?'

(opposite) Alexander 1 of Russia was exceptionally vain and used to apply ice to his face to tighten the skin. He died from typhus in 1825, aged 48, although rumours persisted for many years that he had simply become a monk

The Czar, used to complete subservience in his own domains, was stunned by women who rejected his advances at the Congress. Anna Eynard-Lullin (above) called him an oaf for tearing up her dance card. When he proposed to Countess Julianna Szechenyi (below) that he might occupy her husband's place with her on the dance floor, she retorted: 'Does Your Majesty mistake me for a Polish province?'

Almost as magnificent as the weekly royal ball – and funded indirectly by the same taxes – Metternich's entertainments were perceived as the weather vane of the Congress. The Austrian Chancellor dispensed invitations strictly according to the perceived value of the guests in advancing his political ambitions. The Polish delegation, seeking in vain their country's independence, were rarely on the guest list. However Metternich met his match in Princess Catherine Bagration, the exquisitely formed 31-year-old widow of a Russian general who had died from a gangrenous wound received in 1812 at the Battle of Borodino. Catherine wore clinging dresses made of translucent Indian muslin that left nothing to the imagination. Briefly her lover, fathering an illegitimate daughter, Metternich called her his 'naked angel'. Unfortunately, he soon found she was no longer his. Catherine transferred her affections and sexual skills to Alexander and had the impudence to hold a ball of her own, underwritten, at least the caterers erroneously believed, by the Czar. Although modest in size, it promised to be a magnificent spectacle and was the hottest ticket in town, with only 200 invitees. By an oversight, apparently, Metternich was not invited; but gambling that no one would have the gall to refuse him entry, he went anyway.

The dancing principals at the Congress of Vienna are brilliantly lampooned in this 1814 French cartoon. Talleyrand, one footed, stands on the sidelines (extreme left).
Castlereagh (left, in red) struggles to get off the ground.
Then come Francis of Austria, Alexander of Russia (centre), Frederick William of Prussia and (extreme right) Frederick Augustus of Hanover

Metternich preferred to conduct diplomacy at balls because, he said, half seriously, he felt safer. At his first (and only) one-to-one meeting in private to discuss the future of Poland, the Czar was so acrimonious and threatening towards him, Metternich said afterwards he was not sure whether he would be leaving through the door or the window.

Princess Catherine Bagration, the widow of a Russian general, had a child by Metternich then switched her favours to the Czar. Her exclusive Congress ball, with just 200 invitations, was the hottest ticket in town

After two waltzes, Alexander rudely left his latest mistress standing and sidled up to Karl Auguste von Handenberg, the Prussian Chancellor. If ever a diplomatic turkey had come home to roost, it was the loss to Castlereagh of von Handenberg's skill and support, entirely through the sanctimonious humbug of the British Establishment ruling class. Born in Hanover, the son of a general, he was a loyal subject of King George III, who acted as his mentor, encouraged him to travel, and positioned him to become the Hanoverian representative in London. His appointment in 1773 went well until his young wife, the Countess Reventlow, was discovered in *flagrante delicto* with the incorrigible Prince of Wales.

The society that closed ranks whenever their own discretions threatened to be made public turned savagely on the countess, forcing the von Handenbergs to leave England. Karl was obliged to forge a new career in Prussia, rising through the ranks of civil servants to the top and making himself indispensable to King Wilhelm III. Agreeable and enlightened, he advocated constitutional reforms; which may be why Napoleon disliked him intensely and temporarily forced him out of office. Von Handenberg's marriage in 1772 to the 15-year-old Juliane Reventlow, which ended in divorce, was followed by a string of relationships with young girls, increasingly inappropriate as he approached his dotage. By then von Handenberg was as deaf as a post, so the Czar had to take him out of the ballroom and into his mistress's boudoir to have a private conversation. Seeing what was happening, and fearing a Russian-Prussian rapprochement, Castlereagh and Metternich immediately commandeered the room next door, where they could hear every word of Alexander's raised voice. His new mistress, Princess Bagration, did herself no long term favours by inviting Prince Adam Czartiorysky, the former Russian foreign minister, whom Alexander cut dead on the dance floor. After an eight-year interval apart, the Prince and Empress Elizabeth Alexeievna, lovers from way back, met again at this ball and discreetly rekindled their relationship.

On 16 November, the surfeit of balls proved too much even for the insatiable Russian Czar. Much to Castlereagh's consternation, Alexander was dancing a waltz with Emily when he suddenly collapsed. For one dreadful moment Castlereagh thought his wife had crushed the sacred foot but it turned out Alexander had a recurrence of erysipelas, a skin infection that caused fainting and nausea. He was advised to rest in bed for a week.

On 29 November Alexander and the other sovereigns attended a concert by Ludwig von Beethoven, whose programme included *Wellington's Victory*, a celebration of his success at the Battle of Vitoria, not of course of Waterloo. There was huge applause at the special effects, which included mock cannon fire; although Beethoven's private opinion of this particular example of his work was summed up in one word: *scheisse*. He was a fervent opponent of Bonaparte, not for ideological reasons, but on account of his growing deafness. On the night of 13 May 1809, when the French bombarded Vienna, Beethoven was afraid the noise would destroy what remained of his hearing. He hid in the basement of his brother's house, covering his ears with pillows.

Charles-Joseph, 7th Prince of Ligne, never short of a *bon mot*, quipped that 'Le Congres danse mais il ne marche pas' ('The Congress dances but never takes a forward step'). This was a bit rich coming from a 79-year-old roué who accepted every invitation he received, even if it involved eating five or six dinners a day.

The German composer Ludwig von Beethoven in 1804 (above) and again in 1809 (below). When the French bombarded Vienna, he was afraid the noise would destroy what remained of his hearing; so he hid in the basement of his brother's house, covering his ears with pillows

In December 1814, however, having arranged 'an assignation with a lady' at the weekly Austrian royal ball, he caught a fatal chill while waiting for her at midnight in the cold outside the Hofburg. His funeral, as a former Austrian Field Marshal, impressed even the British delegation accustomed to military ceremonial, a huge and sombre parade led by a black charger carrying Ligne's empty boots reversed in its stirrups. Hundreds of Congress delegates attended but Alexander made only a token appearance, still seething at the late prince's final sally, which mocked the Czar's decidedly eccentric habit of leaving an empty chair for Jesus Christ alongside his invited guests at the dinner table. 'Surely,' said Ligne, 'these feasts cannot all be the Last Supper!'

Almost alone in not having a mistress in Vienna and acutely aware of his disabling absence of dancing skills, Castlereagh fruitlessly complained that diplomacy was 'impeded by this succession of fetes and private Balls – they waste a great deal of valuable time'. In this, however, he was confounded by the French Grand Chamberlain, Charles-Maurice de Talleyrand-Périgord, almost as grand as his name and title. Talleyrand timed to perfection his switch of support to Napoleon during the Emperor's rise to power and just as adroitly had prompted his abdication, prompting Bonaparte to describe him as 'that shit in silk stockings'. To those who questioned his integrity, his regular lining of his own pockets, Talleyrand was always content to counter with his own list of Napoleon's spectacular double-dealing: a Bourbon army officer who had betrayed his oath of loyalty to the king; a Jacobin who sold out the French Revolution; a husband who sacrificed his first wife Josephine on the altar of dynastic ambition. Condemned to sit out the Viennese balls and walking with a pronounced limp due to a lifelong injury to his right foot – he had been dropped as a baby by his wet nurse - Talleyrand devoted his efforts to ensuring that he would not be a bystander in the negotiations that often continued in ante-rooms just off the dance floor. This was no easy task because the Prussians, in particular, wanted to punish France by reducing her territories and her status.

Talleyrand succeeded through the feminine wiles of his niece, at a ball, with a waltz. Duchess Dorothée de Talleyrand-Périgord was estranged from her husband, Edmond de Périgord, and despite the difference in age – almost 40 years - almost certainly was Talleyrand's sexual partner when he took her to Vienna. The French literary critic Charles Sainte-Beuve said she possessed 'eyes with an infernal brilliance' and most men found her extremely alluring. The Prince of Ligne, before the poetic justice of his own demise, had spread the word far and wide about her enchanting looks.

(opposite) The French Grand Chamberlain George-Maurice Talleyrand, described by Napoleon as 'that shit in silk stockings'

Tallyrand was mocked in an 1815 cartoon as 'The Man with Six Heads', a reference to his ability to switch sides and views almost seamlessly

Talleyrand's niece and mistress, Dorothée de Talleyrand-Périgord. Said to possess 'eyes with an infernal brilliance', she helped Talleyrand to regain a place at the negotiating table

During a ball at the Kaunitz Palace, the 21-year-old charmed the Austrian Court. Crown Prince Ferdinand invited Dorothée to partner him in a waltz. Afterwards she presented Talleyrand to Ferdinand, thereby giving him the social status that led, in quick time, to a place back at the top table of nations.

Castlereagh had a taste of what was to come within days, when Talleyrand was invited to comment upon an agreed communiqué drafted by the Foreign Secretary. In it the four great powers were described as 'the Allies'. What did the word mean? asked Talleyrand, with feigned incomprehension. Who were the Allies allied against? Clearly not Napoleon, Emperor of Elba. Clearly not France, with whom the Allies were all now at peace. Castlereagh sighed audibly, took back his document and began again.

Chapter Five

Marshal of the Empire

MANY MONTHS passed and progress remained painfully slow. Early in 1815 Wellington, the ambassador to Paris since Napoleon's abdication, was sent to Austria to replace Castlereagh, ordered back home from Vienna despite his vigorous protests. He was needed to manage a truculent Parliament whose only interest in the Congress seemed to be to complain about its expense. On 1 February Wellington arrived in the Austrian capital by coach, accompanied by a certain Signorina Guiseppina Grassini. At last, a British Ambassador with a mistress, rather than a dull, respectable man seemingly beyond reproach who went shopping with his wife, von Hagen's spies gleefully reported to Metternich. Guiseppina went with him the following evening to a masquerade but to general disappointment, did not remove her mask.

Wellington had been married since April 1806 to Katherine, called Kitty, Packenham, daughter of Baron Longford. In 1792 and 1794 her family ordered Kitty to refuse Wellington's suit, when he had neither sufficient assets nor, it seemed at the time, good career prospects. Wellington took rejection badly and in a fit of self-recrimination even burned his favourite possession, his father's violin. Twelve years later he proposed again, by letter, and after much agonising Kitty broke off a rival engagement. The couple met less than a week before their wedding when Wellington discovered that Kitty, now aged 34, had not worn well. He confided to his brother Richard, 'By Jove she's grown ugly!' The marriage produced two children but was not a success. Wellington found Kitty to be stubborn, inclined to argue her corner to the point of exhaustion; generous with money they did not possess, incapable of managing the household accounts; and an insatiable gossip who could never be trusted with a military secret. Within weeks of setting up home in London's Harley Street, they had moved back into separate bedrooms.

(opposite) Guissepina Grassini, a voluptuous Italian contralto. Guissepina became mistress to both Napoleon and Wellington, although not at the same time

Katherine, or Kitty, Packenham, wife of the Duke of Wellington. Her family made Kitty reject Wellington twice when she was in her prime. When Wellington next saw Kitty just before the wedding day, he confided in his brother, 'My Jove she's grown ugly!

'La Grassini' for Wellington was no ordinary dalliance. Born in Varese, near Milan, she was one of the finest contraltos in Europe, performing several times in London at the Haymarket Theatre between 1803 and 1806. After her return to Paris, Napoleon made her his leading court singer and also his mistress. The voluptuous Guiseppina loved presents. Napoleon gave her a silver snuff box covered in diamonds. In 1814, Wellington, his successor for the Grassini's favours, brought her a more modest broach. Guiseppina had only a smattering of English, not much French to speak of and hardly understood a word her 'dear Villainton' said; but later she reminisced with a wicked smile, 'we got on well, all the same!'

Wellington had barely settled in Vienna when, eight days after the Congress had issued what everyone hoped would be its final report, Bonaparte disappeared from Elba. The chain of events that prompted his escape began with Elizabeth

Vassall Fox, a lady snubbed by the Almack's entry committee because of what they considered to be her scandalous behaviour: she had a son out of wedlock. Born in Jamaica, the daughter of a rich planter from Britain's American colonies, in 1786 Elizabeth Vassall, aged just 15, became the reluctant bride of Sir Godfrey Webster, 4th Baronet. He was interested only in the size of her inheritance and it proved a disastrous marriage. In 1793 she embarked on a passionate love affair with the 3rd Lord Holland, Henry Fox, nephew of the Whigs leader Charles James Fox, after they had met at a ball in Florence. Sir Godfrey divorced Elizabeth in 1797 on the grounds of her adultery and went quickly through the £6,000 settlement. Three years later, no longer able to get his hands on any of her money to pay his growing gambling debts, in desperation he shot himself in his study. Although Lord Holland and Elizabeth married and he acknowledged his son Charles, still Almack's patronesses would not receive her. The new Lady Holland set up a rival salon at Holland House, a magnificent mansion with 200 acres of grounds near London's present-day Earl's Court. From 1813 Elizabeth held glittering balls in direct competition to Almack's. Here in contrast the hopeful offspring of society ladies, denied what their mothers regarded as the first prize of an Almack's season ticket, could dance the forbidden waltz to their heart's content with the beau of their choice.

The guest list at Holland House, usually a hot-bed of Whig opposition and sympathisers of Napoleon, nonetheless included some illustrious names: Metternich, the Czar and Talleyrand. Even they discovered Lady Holland displayed little of the deference usually taken for granted. On the contrary, she was a formidable hostess of domineering arrogance and breath-taking rudeness. Her husband was putty in her hands. She told him when to go to bed, what to wear and ordered servants to escort him from the dinner table if he dared to interrupt.

During the uneasy peace between Britain and France that followed the Treaty of Amiens in 1801, Napoleon had received Lady Holland graciously in Paris. Thereafter she was a fervent Bonapartist, contemptuously dismissive of the nuances of British foreign policy. When the deposed Napoleon's promised annual pension of 2.5 million francs predictably failed to arrive from the new Bourbon administration, she sent money and food to him in Elba and hundreds of books; but above all a regular supply of British, US and European newspapers. Among them were copies of a popular London evening, *The Courier*, in particular its edition of 19 October 1814 – by a curious coincidence, the date of the first public airing across the Atlantic of the *Star Studied Banner*. Napoleon learned from a brief report that the Congress regarded his exile to Elba as a temporary expedient. According to The Courier, Castlereagh had suggested as an alternative, not the freedom-loving America as he had unrealistically hoped, but the remote British possession of St. Helena, an island in the South Atlantic.

Elizabeth Vassall Fox, Lady Holland, who was refused an entry ticket to Almack's because she had a child out of wedlock. Lady Holland started rival balls at Holland House that included the waltz, still banned at Almack's as unseemly

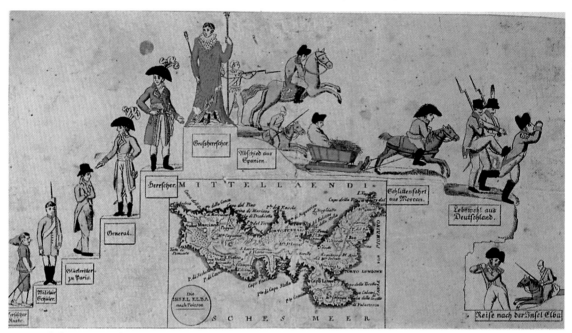

'The Rise and Fall of Napoleon' produced in April 1814 by the German political cartoonist, Johann Voltz, with the island of Elba inserted.
Napoleon's story had one more dramatic chapter to come

Thus forewarned and accordingly bringing forward his plans to escape, Bonaparte fraternised with the crews of the British naval vessels sent to keep an eye on him. Although the Admiralty was not amused, and not long afterwards 'beached' him on half pay for 22 years, Captain John Tower even placed a throne on deck when the Emperor attended a ball held on board the frigate HMS Curacao. According to Tower, Napoleon danced the waltz and despite being conspicuously overweight, gallantly attempted the hornpipe. Back ashore, he was soon running rings around Sir Neil Campbell, the dour Scottish colonel sent by Castlereagh to Elba as British Commissioner, with a knighthood as the carrot. Not a lucky soldier – at the battle of La Fère-Champenoise he was slashed beneath the left eye by the member of a Cossack patrol mistaking him for a French officer – Campbell was given an impossible brief to watch but not curb the activities of a man who had the luck of the devil. However, Campbell fell victim to one of the oldest tricks in the book: a honey trap almost certainly devised by one of Napoleon's spies in Livorno.

The suave, sophisticated comtessa Elena Minaccia, who had fluttered her eyelids at him on the deck of HMS Curacao, possessed apparently impeccable credentials. She appeared on the VIP guest list of John Fane, Lord Burghersh,

British Minister Plenipotentiary to the Royal Court in Florence. Burghersh had served as aide-de-camp with Wellington in the peninsula campaign. His rapid promotion to lieutenant-colonel over the heads of 600 other officers caused uproar in the House of Commons. While remaining nominally on active military service, Burghersh diligently promoted British diplomatic interests among the Florentine nobility by arranging a whole series of concerts that began with performances of the operas he himself had composed.

Sir Neil Campbell, the British Commissioner on Elba, was lured away to Florence by a honey trap.
While he danced with an Italian comtessa at a ball in the British Embassy, Napoleon set sail for France

Livorno (known as Leghorn in England) and Florence were both part of the Napoleonic kingdom of Etruria, where many Bonaparte sympathisers remained

(previous page) Napoleon's departure from Elba as seen by Joseph Beaume.
To avoid arousing suspicion, he left straight after attending a carnival ball held at the
Teatro dei Vigilanti in the capital, Portoferraio

In contrast, like most members of the British officer class, Campbell spent his spare time drinking, gambling and whoring and had little or no interest in cultural pursuits. It was the forbidden fruits offered by the comtessa that took him by the British frigate *HMS Partridge* to Livorno, from where he travelled by coach to Florence to attend what was described as an 'opera ball' at the British Embassy. According to the local *Gazzetta*, on Saturday, 25 February 1815 the 'elegant guests…were served sumptuous refreshments… typical of Lord Burghersh's usual magnificence'. The opera began at 5 p.m. and lasted four hours, supper a further two, and carriages after the ball itself were due at 3 a.m. The newspaper diary item does not shed any light on whether Elena then succumbed to her aspiring lover but the comtessa – if indeed she were a countess at all – had kept Campbell away from Elba at the vital moment. A day later Napoleon sailed for France. Campbell returned to *HMS Partridge*, awaiting his pleasure anchored at Livorno. He soon learned of Bonaparte's audacious escape but his frantic but less than hot pursuit ended in fiasco when his ship became becalmed.

On 1 March the Emperor and his little army spent the night under the stars at Cannes near the present day Croisette. They were accidentally serenaded by the band of the provincial governor and oblivious to the potentially mortal threat posed by a local butcher, who had to be persuaded by his customers to abandon his plan to shoot Napoleon with his ancient musket. The myth of the Emperor's advance inland via what is now known the 'Route Napoleon' grew in the telling. However, he reached the outskirts of Grenoble without the forces he needed to seize the city, still less the momentum to take him all the way to Paris. Not a single Bourbon officer joined Napoleon until he arrived at a small hamlet named Vizille, where Colonel Charles François Huchet de la Bédoyère had his moment in history.

La Bédoyère, while undoubtedly dashing and debonair, was also a combination of the real d'Artagnan and the fictitious Richard Sharpe: fearless, famous and foolish. His survival (albeit often wounded) on the battlefield, given the risks he took, was against all odds. His propensity to disobey orders, to misread the politics of a situation, was bound to get him into serious trouble sooner or later.

Charles was a Breton born in Paris, the son of Charles Marie Philippe Huchet, comte de la Bédoyère, a minor noble and magistrate. In 1806, aged 20, he responded to Napoleon's call to the nobility to join his victorious army.

Charles de la Bédoyère was a combination of the real d'Artagnan and the fictitious Richard Sharpe: fearless, famous and foolish

Charles junior rose through the ranks of the Imperial Guard. As the aide-de-camp to one of the best of Napoleon's marshals, Jean Lannes, he occasionally came into personal contact with the Emperor. But he was far from a pampered staff officer content to be safe from the field of battle. In April 1809 the French attack on the citadel of Regensburg using scaling ladders faltered under withering enemy fire. La Bédoyère, showing almost suicidal courage, climbed a ladder on his own and shamed others into following him. A month later Lannes lost both legs to a cannonball at the Battle of Aspern-Essling and died shortly afterwards; but la Bédoyère became aide-de-camp instead to Napoleon's stepson, Prince Eugène, and followed him to Italy.

(previous page) The Battle of Regensburg, April 1809. When a French attack faltered, la Bédoyère climbed one of the scaling ladders himself, shaming his men into following him

In August 1810 the Chastellux left Paris for a summer holiday at the chateau of Luc-le-Bois, the home of a junior branch of the family and in particular of another of those extraordinary women who contributed to this kaleidoscope of momentous events. The almost indestructible 'Miss Plunkett', as she insisted on being called, although born at Louvain in modern-day Belgium, where her Irish father had been in Austrian military service, lived to the great age of 97. In her role as Marie Josephine Charlotte Brigitte, marquise de Chastellux, widow of Francois Jean, marquis de Chastellux, she exchanged letters with President Thomas Jefferson himself in vain search of a pension for the marquis's timely help during the American War of Independence. Marie believed strongly in the social emancipation of women, and the political emancipation of men. She berated the three unmarried Chastellux daughters for allowing their parents to choose their future husbands. She also corresponded about politics with their distant cousin, the very same Charles de la Bédoyère. She discovered that despite his career in the army, he was a man of letters, who had regularly visited the salon of Anne-Louise Germaine Necker, better known as Madame de Staële.

Marie, Marquise de Chastellux, always known as 'Miss Plunkett', was the daughter of an Irish mercenary. La Bédoyère's mentor, she encouraged his rebellious and revolutionary ideas

On Saturday 22 June 1811, her two causes conveniently converged. La Bédoyère was invited to attend a ball at Thil, the Chastellux's principal country estate and chateau west of Dijon in Burgundy. Despite his respectable parentage, Charles came under intense scrutiny. He was rumoured to be a gambler and a womaniser, perhaps, despite his legendary status as a soldier, not quite the ideal husband for Judith, Pauline or Georgine Victoire. Nor was it love at first sight.

The Chateau de Thil, the Chastellux's principal country estate west of Dijon in Burgundy. It was here at a ball that la Bédoyère first met and wooed the youngest of the Chastellux daughters

After much dancing and romancing, Charles could not decide between the three eligible young ladies, irritating his father and prompting a sharp note from Miss Plunkett. She told him to stop prevaricating and propose to her favourite, Georgine, the youngest in the family. Georgine accepted him graciously but their wedding plans came to an abrupt halt the following June, when la Bédoyère was summoned to join the vast army of 422,000 men assembled for the French invasion of Russia.

The preparations for this daunting enterprise were never realistic. Napoleon took with him only enough supplies for a three-week campaign and had no winter shoes with spikes for his horses. After waiting in the ruins of Moscow for a surrender that never came, in October he was forced into a disastrous retreat as winter closed in. Perhaps as few as 10,000 of his troops survived as an effective force, amid terrible scenes of abandoned equipment, cannibalism, desperate men and animals, more akin to the Apocalypse. One of la Bédoyère's friends, the Belgian François Dumonceau, recalled how he had no option but to lead his horse over 'a veritable moving mountain, more than two metres deep, of dead and dying, pushing, shoving, hemmed in on all sides, at each step risking being thrown down by the convulsive spasms of those we were trampling underfoot'. La Bédoyère was among those who fought heroically to enable the survivors to cross the Berezina River into Poland on two wooden pontoon bridges.

(previous page) The famous picture by Aldolphe Yvon of Marshal Ney (centre) supporting the Rear Guard during the Retreat from Moscow. Barely 10,000 of Napoleon's 422,000 strong army survived as a fighting force after a nightmare journey

On 23 August 1813 Charles, newly promoted to colonel, was badly wounded, shot in the left thigh, during a skirmish in Silesia. His return to Thil on convalescent leave prompted scenes of wild rejoicing, as he had been reported dead. His marriage to Georgine, postponed many times, finally took place on 23 November at Paris in a chapel off the rue du Bac. Without horses for most of his surviving cavalry, Napoleon suffered defeat after defeat. As the hopeless struggle against the far superior numbers of the allied armies came closer to the capital,

The wedding portraits of Charles de la Bédoyère and Georgine de Chastellux, who married in Paris in November 1813

Georgine saw more of her husband, one of the last to give up the struggle. On Wednesday, 31 March 1814, just before the armistice, cannon fire was clearly audible from the direction of Montmartre, where the Prussians were attacking and la Bédoyère was in charge of the defence. In the middle of dinner, Georgine heard a horse enter the courtyard at a gallop. It was her husband. Rushing out to greet him, she saw Charles swaying with fatigue, wearing a uniform covered in blood (fortunately not his own), and desperate for water. She led him inside, stripped off his clothes and ignoring the sensitivities of the period, took him to bed. They made love tenderly for three hours. At 10.30 p.m. la Bédoyère got back on his horse and went back into battle.

Under the Bourbons, Charles soon found what it meant to belong to an ultra-royalist family. They strongly disapproved of his principled resignation from the army following Napoleon's abdication and were even more indignant when he turned down an offer to become a senior officer in Louis XVIII's' bodyguard. La Bédoyère had a blazing row with his father-in-law, who effectively forced him to accept a new commission. On October 4 1814 he became colonel of the Seventh Line regiment quartered at Chambéry but remained on leave because of his wife's advanced pregnancy. His son, baptised Georges-Cesar-Raphael, was born three weeks later but the following February la Bédoyère still showed no sign of taking up his post. Only after a direct order from General Marchand on 22 February 1815 did he set out from Paris for Chambéry, reporting for duty four days later.

News of Napoleon's escape reached Chambéry on the evening of 5 March. The following day la Bédoyère, ordered to move his regiment to intercept, stopped for lunch at an inn run by a certain Madame de Bellegarde. Afterwards, as he came outside and remounted he called out to his host, 'Goodbye Madam, in eight days either I will be shot or I will be a Marshal of the Empire!' His men thought he was joking but he was half serious. This typical piece of hyperbole from a man always larger than life would slip a proverbial noose around his neck. La Bédoyère continued south, past Grenoble and onwards for a further seven kilometres, almost to the little town of Vizille, which had a particular resonance in the French Revolution. It was here, on 21 July 1788, that 491 members of the local Estates, a long defunct multi-tiered ineffectual assembly, finally had been allowed to meet and opposition to absolute monarchy came out into the open. Thanks to the teachings of Miss Plunkett, Charles was well aware of its great significance. He took up a position at the head of his column, the tramp of their boots and the click of bayonet on rifle audible to the Emperor's tiny force, still many hundreds of metres away.

Suddenly la Bédoyère calls halt and turns to face his men. He unfurls an eagle, his regiment's former and now forbidden standard, which he had found at Chambéry, stuffed in a box. In a clear resounding voice he declares for Napoleon and adds, 'Qui m'aime me suit!' ('Who loves me follows me!') It is the ringing 14th century chivalric cry of Philippe VI of Valois, reused inspirationally across the centuries. There are wild cheers of 'Vive L'Emperor!' The commotion is heard by la Bédoyère's commanding officer, General Devilliers, who comes galloping up. Incredulous at what has happened, he pleads with Charles to think again, to think of his future. La Bédoyère's only response is to invite him to address the regiment. Sixty men, the most timid, return with the general to Grenoble. The rest are in a heady state of supreme exultation. Charles puts his eagle on the

*Two pivotal events in French history were played out at the tiny town of Vizille.
In 1788, local representatives manifested the first organised opposition to the Bourbons
absolute monarchy. In 1815, Charles de la Bédoyère became the first officer in the Bourbon
army to declare for Napoleon*

tip of a convenient stick and orders a drummer to beat the time of the march. At long last, Napoleon himself comes into view. La Bédoyère seizes the side drum, symbolically smashes its stretched drum skin top, and presents the eagle to the Emperor. Napoleon embraces him. The die is cast.

Strangely, Andrew Roberts in his magnificent biography *Napoleon the Great* elects to give only a single line to this pivotal episode. Charles chose to go with his heart rather than his head at a moment when Napoleon's return hung in the balance. It horrified the Chastellux, especially la Bédoyère's brother-in-law Henry Louis, aged 28, affluent, with a comfortable posting attached to the French embassy in Rome. When he heard the news, he threw diplomatic papers, money and clothes into the back of his private coach and set out for Genoa to take ship to Nice, somehow convinced he could catch up with la Bédoyère and talk him out of his folly. Only later would he discover that one of the other guests at Georgine's wedding, the comtesse de Boigne, had done exactly the opposite. She was well aware what a rabid Bonapartiste Charles really was, always hoping for the Emperor's return. Adélaïde Charlotte Louise Éléonore Osmond was a soldier's daughter, born and brought up in the Palace of Versailles but like Miss Plunkett, Irish blood flowed proudly through her veins. The comtesse's grandfather was Robert Dillon, an Irishman wanted by the British. She had married the fabulously wealthy comte de Boigne while both were in exile in England, only to find that he also had an Indian wife and two children, abandoned in the sub-continent where he had made his fortune. Both ladies disliked the return of the Old Regime, where women were expected to bite their tongues, and thought France a better place for the fairer sex under Napoleon.

What went almost unnoticed by the traumatised Chastellux was that even while the Emperor was reviewing his men drawn up outside Vizille, Charles, walking beside him, bent Bonaparte's ear on the need for constitutional reforms. He did not want a dictator, however benevolent and beloved, back in charge. Napoleon reassured him and made promises that he broke as soon as he reached Lyon. It was only in May, when war became inevitable, at the third time of asking that la Bédoyère accepted the Emperor's offer of promotion to general de brigade. 'You owe me nothing,' had been his immediate response at Vizille. Within hours the cowardly prefect of Grenoble scurried north to safety, abandoning the city. Bonaparte now had 7,000 troops at his disposal. Taking command of the advance guard, General Cambronne expressed concern at the shortage of cartridges. 'You won't be needing any', was Napoleon's confident reply.

On 5 March the Chappe telegraph system, which could send messages more than 250 miles in a single day, warned the royal family in Paris of Napoleon's unstoppable progress. When the news reached Vienna on 7 March, an imperial

Charlotte Osmond, comtesse de Boigne, was the second titled lady of Irish descent to influence la Bédoyère. Her grandfather had been wanted by the British

orchestra was playing at a tea dance, seated on a balcony behind a wrought iron balustrade made from discarded French muskets, following what everyone had assumed to be the Emperor's decisive defeat at Leipzig. The violinists, halfway through a waltz, tailed off in confusion when they realised everyone had stopped dancing, as the sensational story of Napoleon's return spread like lightning. 'Why did you let him escape?' demanded the irate Alexander. 'Why did you send him to Elba?' responded Wellington, laconically. The Congress hastily reconvened and declared 'The Grand Disturber' an outlaw, with a price on his head.

Lady Holland's own plans to visit Elba were frustrated by Napoleon's escape. According to her hen-pecked husband, sotto voce to a dependable friend, this news set her 'spirits in such a flurry and agitation that I suppose she will not be calm and sedate enough to enjoy the improving gravity of Doric architecture'. Castlereagh was forced to deny in the Commons that there had been any plan for removing Napoleon from Elba, blaming it on 'an unauthorised and groundless paragraph in a newspaper', an all-too familiar style of rebuttal that would stand the test of time. The obvious scapegoat, Campbell, hotly denied allegations that he had been bribed but Admiral Lord Exmouth, criticised for the inept performance of the Royal Navy, shifted the blame and contrived to have the soldier-diplomat sent home in disgrace for 'misusing one of His Majesty's ships of the line'.

(previous page) 'The fox and the goose; or Boney let loose': George Cruikshank's interpretation of Napoleon's return to power in 1815. Bonaparte is the fox; the allies, still deliberating at the Congress of Vienna (top left,) are the geese. Entertainment remains their priority, a ball at 8 p.m., preceded by a 'Bull Bait' at 4 p.m., a fight between a lion and several huge Hungarian bull mastiffs. Such blood sports took place regularly in the Vienna amphitheatre – and in England, where the last on record was held at Warwick in 1825.

Chapter Six

The Wash-House

THE BOURBONS packed their bags and left Paris only a few hours before Napoleon reached the palace of Fontainebleau. The gout-ridden Louis XVIII was so convinced that the Emperor would sweep all before him, the British government had great difficulty in persuading him to re-establish his Court at Ghent in the Netherlands rather than cross the English Channel. He was followed by British residents in the French capital with more dignity and less haste, as far as Brussels, which already had a thriving British community.

Brussels in 1815, still a walled city. It had 1,500 British residents but most of its inhabitants hoped for the return of Napoleon

At its head were the Duke and Duchess of Richmond, destined, but for a certain village called Waterloo and a ball in a barn, to a peripheral role in all but the most obscure of histories. The Duke of Richmond, George Lennox, was a convivial but prickly dolt, who came within a whisker of being sentenced to hang, had he killed his intended target in a duel, a member of the royal family, Frederick, Duke of York. This was the duke whose indecision in battle during the early Napoleonic wars resulted in this ironic refrain:

> *The grand old Duke of York,*
> *He had ten thousand men.*
> *He marched them up to the top of the hill*
> *And he marched them down again.*
> *And when they were up, they were up.*
> *And when they were down, they were down.*
> *And when they were only halfway up,*
> *They were neither up nor down.*

On 15 May 1789, just before the French Revolution, Lennox, a lieutenant-colonel at the time, and Frederick, his commanding officer, went separately to a masked ball at Daubigney's Club in London. George's uncle had only illegitimate offspring by his housekeeper and as heir apparent to a dukedom, Lennox behaved as though he was Frederick's equal. The royal duke, safely concealed behind a mask, took the opportunity to tell Lennox exactly what he thought of him; he did not bargain on Lennox relentlessly pinning down his identity afterwards and demanding satisfaction. On 26 May they met in a duel on Wimbledon Common. Lennox fired on the given signal, his pistol ball grazing the Duke of York's forehead and flicking a curl on his wig, demonstrating the seriousness of his intentions. The royal duke lowered his pistol and quietly said he had no intention of firing. The duel was over but the affair rumbled on. Lennox saw no reason not to take up his invitation to a ball held shortly afterwards at Buckingham House to celebrate Queen Charlotte's birthday. The Prince of Wales opened an English country dance with the Princess Royal but deliberately left Lennox and his partner out of sequence and when it was their turn to lead, as they came down between the rows of waiting dancers he took the princess off the floor. The prince expressed his indignation at Lennox's presence to Queen Charlotte, who retired with her ladies. At that point, according to memorialist William Wallace, 'the ball broke up with the same abruptness as the banquet in Macbeth'.

The Coldstream Guards held an enquiry into the duel that concluded Lennox had 'behaved with courage, but…not with judgment' and in July he was transferred to a socially inferior regiment, the 35th foot, stationed in Edinburgh. Here he rekindled his relationship with Lady Charlotte Gordon, supposedly the eldest daughter of Alexander, 4th Duke of Gordon. Charlotte had been

The ROYAL DUEL.

A London printer rushed out a cartoon of 'The Royal Duel' within 24 hours of the occasion in May 1789. Although it shows the Duke of York (right) firing into the air rather than take aim at George Lennox (left), in reality the duke refused to discharge his pistol

presented at court that summer and attended the masked ball during her visit to London without the knowledge and approval of her mother, Jane Maxwell, Duchess of Gordon. Both the mature Gordons were extremely promiscuous: Alexander sired ten bastards and his wife had desperately assured one of her daughter's suitors, a close cousin concerned about consanguinity, that Charlotte had 'not a drop of the Duke's blood in her'. What Charlotte thought she had, come early September, was an unmistakeable indication that she was pregnant; and although in due course this turned out to be a false alarm, her mother took no chances. On 9 September 1789, George and Charlotte were married at a bizarre ceremony conducted in the Duchess of Gordon's dressing room at Gordon Castle, with two parlour maids as witnesses, and the announcement made only at a dinner party three days later. The couple had a great deal of sex, resulting in fourteen healthy children in nineteen years. They lost only one, and not from natural causes. In February 1812, while serving on HMS Blake as a midshipman, the 14-year-old Henry Lennox fell from the mast into the sea and was drowned.

In September 1789 George Lennox, the future Duke of Richmond, a convivial but prickly dolt, married Lady Charlotte Gordon, irascible, blinkered and domineering, in indecent haste. At the time Charlotte feared that she might be pregnant

In 1806 George succeeded to the dukedom and the following year was appointed Lord Lieutenant of Ireland in Dublin where Arthur Wellesley, temporarily short of a command, acted as his Chief Secretary. All seemed set fair until 1809, when the Duke of Richmond wrote an extremely compromising letter to Lady Augusta Everitt, with whom he was having an affair. He omitted to explain with sufficient clarity to a dim-witted footman that it was to be delivered to his mistress, not to the mistress of the house. William Congreve's description of "Hell a Fury, like a Woman scorn'd" did not do justice to Charlotte's reaction when she read its contents. George was banished forever from the marital bedroom and drowned his sorrows in port. It was universally acknowledged by everyone that the Duchess's 'Temper is dreadful' and her boys' young tutor, Spencer Madan, said 'she is one of the sourest most ill-tempered personages I ever came across… one day she was angry because she did not receive a letter from the Duke, another because she did'.

The Duchess of Richmond's humour was not improved by their desperate financial situation. The dukedom brought with it Richmond House in London and a country estate at Goodwood in Sussex but also about £180,000 in debts, perhaps £7M in modern money. When the duke and duchess left Ireland for England in 1813, having lavishly entertained in Dublin, another £50,000 of debt had been accumulated. Their only option was to find a solution that avoided the looming bankruptcy but still enabled Charlotte to save face. In June 1814 Richmond wrote to his friend, the Honourable John Capel, about following his example and coming to Brussels with his family 'for a year on an Economical Plan'. There was no time to lose and Richmond, accompanied by his two eldest daughters, Mary and Sarah, arrived within a matter of weeks. They rented a property, No. 23 rue de la Blanchisserie, described by Lady Caroline Capel as a 'delightful house and gardens in the Lower part of the town'. She added, however, a socially crushing reservation, '…and delightful it ought to be, to at all compensate for the disadvantage of the situation', a comment that left Richmond in abject terror of what his wife would think upon her arrival.

The weeks passed all too swiftly. On 28 August the Duchess and her entourage of seventeen in two coaches, including seven children, four maids and Mr Alfred Johnson the butler, set out from London to Deal. Richmond had pulled strings and HMS Redpole, a 10-gun sloop that would end its days sunk by pirates, was diverted to pick them up. The weather, alas, had other ideas. They did not set sail until 5 September, arriving off Ostende at 8 p.m. but in seas too rough to make harbour. Reckless though it was, Charlotte, terribly seasick, insisted on everyone being taken ashore by rowing boat, and at low tide, which meant they had to walk for miles along the beach to the nearest inn. On 14 September, sixteen days after leaving London, they finally arrived in Brussels, with the Duchess in the worst of humour.

Her new address, an 18th century mansion in a street close to the Blanchisserie de la Fontaine, the Fountain Laundry, named after a small spring at the end of the street, was a source of acute embarrassment to Charlotte. Her address was soon exploited relentlessly by the Duke of Wellington, who insisted on calling it 'the Wash-House'. On the east side it even had an actual pump and wash-house in the grounds, covered in tiles. On the south side it was bordered by the van Ginderachter Brewery, whose gurgling vats could be heard night and day. Still, beggars could not be choosers, and at least the property had ample room for all the servants and, most important for the Duchess, a large annexe. Measuring 13 by 16 metres, although only 4 metres high, it had been used by Jean Simons to display examples of the products of his highly successful luxury coach-building business. His customers had included the Emperor Napoleon himself, although he never paid the bill. His son Michel-Jean, whose card described himself as a 'stationery supplier', squandered the profits on his mistress, Anne-Francoise Elisabeth Lange. Born in Genoa of a French musician and an Italian actress, Mademoiselle Lange had performed with distinction at the Comédie Française in Paris. At the height of the Terror, she survived a brief term of imprisonment after incurring the wrath of the Committee of Public Safety for her bawdy performance in *Pamela*. She proved, however, an extremely expensive catch and the besotted coachbuilder, almost as deep in debt as the Richmonds, was forced to rent out his Brussels property. The Richmonds were Michel-Jean's first tenants. Charlotte turned the annexe, complete with its hideous wallpaper of trellis and roses, into a schoolroom and playroom for her younger daughters, where battledore and shuttlecock were favoured on a wet day. It would also become the venue for the most famous ball in history.

The annexe to the Brussels house rented by the Duke and Duchess of Richmond in 1815. Formerly used to display newly constructed coaches to potential customers, it became the insalubrious venue of the most famous ball in history

(opposite) The French actress Anne-Françoise Lange in the role of Danáê from Greek mythology, whose extravagance forced her lover, Michel-Jean Simons, to rent out his house in Brussels to make ends meet. The Richmonds were his first clients

For the time being, ordinary Brussels balls were two a penny. With almost 1,500 civilian British ex-patriots in the capital of the former Austrian Netherlands, and as many other foreigners, several took place nearly every week. The Duchess held a 'Regency Rout' for 180 guests on 12 November, noted at the time for its penny-pinching supper. When others were entertaining, she was usually the first to arrive and the last to depart, seeming to require very little sleep. The Prince of Orange, invested with the Order of the Garter by Castlereagh, on his way back to Vienna, rather presumptuously gave a ball in honour of himself. His son, the Hereditary Prince William Frederick of Orange, not to be outdone, announced a 'Grand Masked Ball and Supper'. It was held on Monday 13 February 1815 and opened with a huge quadrille in which the prince featured prominently, having practised its steps for weeks. The 600 guests 'were dressed in superb and handsome style', all in local satins (much cheaper than London). Not altogether out of character, the Duchess of Richmond went 'as a poor woman with a basket of eggs'.

However it was the waltz, not the quadrille, which caused controversy. The Duchess at first refused to allow it to be included at her own entertainments She was supported by the 33-year-old English pastor from Welton Brinkham in Lincolnshire, the Reverend George Griffin Stonestreet, chaplain to the Brigade of Guards. He described the faster variations of the waltz as a 'completely indecent and violent romp'. Richmond, on Charlotte's instructions, ordered his daughters not to dance the waltz at other balls but they defied him on frequent occasions. By May, even the Duchess had been forced to admit defeat.

Meanwhile Wellington was still in Vienna, finding no shortage of proposals to send massed armies against France, but always at a price. News that Russia was raising 200,000 men in Würzburg worried the Austrians far more than Bonaparte's return. The Prussians assimilated troops from Saxony, who promptly mutinied. They tried hard to persuade Wellington to hand over control of his Hanoverian regiments, without success. On behalf of the British government, Wellington agreed to pay up to £7 million, a staggering sum, to the allies in lieu of its proportionate contribution of soldiers. He was appointed commander-in-chief of allied forces in the new Kingdom of the Netherlands, at that stage largely a paper army, in a country hopelessly divided on political, religious and linguistic grounds. Wellington was impatient to leave Vienna. On 29 March, accompanied by his ADC, one of Richmond's sons, Lieutenant William Lennox, he rode hell for leather across Europe and arrived in Brussels on 4 April, 24 hours ahead of a courier bearing dispatches from the Congress.

Wellington had a polyglot army to organise, something akin to a forerunner of NATO, but with little in the way of credible intelligence reports about the whereabouts of the enemy. Great Britain had declared war on Napoleon but not yet on France, so his forces were obliged to remain north of the border. He made sure, however, that the terrain south of Brussels was scouted thoroughly, as a suitable location for a defensive position against superior numbers. The fact that the nearest village happened to be called Waterloo, Wellington neither knew nor cared.

What he did was to put on an act of such insouciance that it convinced his fellow officers as well as the network of informers who could slip across the frontier and send messages guaranteed to be in Napoleon's hands in Paris a few days later. Wellington attended a huge number of public and private events in the Netherlands, as if he had not a care in the world. They included several cricket matches organised by Richmond, a talented batsman and wicketkeeper. He had offered a financial guarantee to Thomas Lord to help him found Lord's cricket ground in north London. Wellington even occasionally put on his pads himself, despite a decidedly poor batting average of his own. In recognised fixtures he had scored just 6 runs in 2 innings, playing in August 1792 (as the Hon. A. Wesby on the score sheet) for a so-called 'All Ireland' side against 'The Garrison' in Dublin.

The 15-year-old William Lennox had been fielding on the boundary at Enghien when his fellow cricketers persuaded him for a bet to ride an ill-trained Cossack horse around the lake. The horse bolted, throwing Lennox against a tree. He was left in a coma, his skull fractured and his right arm broken in two places. After three days hovering between life and death, he sat up and asked where he was. William had lost his sight in his right eye and remained on the sick list for two months.

His commander-in-chief made a point of being seen at race meetings and picnics, at parties and parades. He remained so outwardly imperturbable that the local population and the British exiles became convinced there was no need for them to worry. Major-General Lord Edward Somerset wrote home to say that the advance into France was not expected until 26 June. 'In the meantime the Duke of Wellington is very gay at Brussels and gives a great Ball and supper at least once a week.' But behind the scenes Wellington was working feverishly to bring experienced British troops back from America and re-form regiments who had returned to England from the Peninsular War so they could be sent across the Channel.

In no way a pretence, however, was Wellington's insatiable need for women. The Richmonds' private tutor, Madan, suspected an ulterior motive when the Duke, just short of his 46th birthday, devoted a great deal of time to their 16-year-old daughter, Lady Jane Lennox. He took her to a Guards cricket match at Enghien 'apparently… for no other purpose than to amuse her', Madan disapprovingly reported, noting that their return to the rue de la Blanchisserie came late at night, long after stumps had been drawn. This rather unsavoury dalliance was soon superseded, however, by the Duke's passionate desire for the Irish-born Lady Frances Caroline Wedderburn Webster.

She was the daughter of the 1st Earl of Mountnorris and the 21-year-old wife of James Wedderburn Webster. James was a considerable athlete and an inveterate gambler, known as 'Bold Webster'. He once successfully wagered 600 guineas that he could beat the clock on his phaeton mare, *Buzzard*, between London's Westminster Bridge and the Royal Stables and Riding House in Brighton, recording 3 hours 20 minutes, an average of over 16 miles per hour. Both he, and *Buzzard*, were refreshed by a large glass of red wine at the halfway point.

The Websters' marriage in 1810 was one of convenience, not love. Frances was desperate to escape her family while James, having made his money in trade, simply coveted the respectability of her title. Frances took several lovers, including her husband's drinking pal, Lord Byron. In 1811 she attracted gossip by calling her first-born son 'Byron'; he died in infancy. After the Websters, too, became economic exiles in Brussels, Frances met Wellington at a dinner party organised by the Richmonds. She was already pregnant again, about five months into term – her second son would be born in Paris on 28 August 1815 – but her growing belly evidently did not present the Duke with a serious obstacle to sexual intercourse.

With her husband safely away on business on the other side of the Channel, Wellington saw no reason for concealment, except, that is, in a secluded wooded copse deep inside a Brussels park, where the passionate pair were nearly caught by Frances's suspicious elderly mother.

Lady Frances Wedderburn Webster, heavily pregnant but still highly promiscuous, embarked on a rampant affair with the Duke of Wellington in Brussels

Fortunately for them Lady Mountnorris, arriving at the park after her daughter in of course a different coach, one that had to be driven gently because of a broken spring, had neither the eyes quite to see between the trees nor the legs to pursue.

On 26 April Wellington gave a grand ball. The aide-de-camp to Lieutenant-General Lord Rowland Hill, Captain Sir Digby Mackworth, had this to say about it: 'The Duke himself danced, and always with the same person, a Lady Frances Webster, to whom he paid so much attention, that Scandal, who is become Goddess here, began to whisper all sorts of stories'. Mackworth, almost alone of the officers billeted in Brussels, was not energetically pursuing the opposite sex and had quite a story of his own to tell. Taken prisoner in Spain and sent to France, he had fallen in love with his jailer's daughter, the Baroness Julie de Richepanse, but was compelled to leave her behind when he was repatriated to England in an exchange. Reunited after Waterloo, they married in September 1816, only for his wife, after the difficult birth of their son, to die tragically in March 1818.

Chapter Seven

The Spy at the Duchess's Ball

CAPTAIN GRONOW seemed destined to kick his heels in London, guarding St James' Palace, while deeds of derring-do were about to happen on the Continent. But over dinner he happened to meet Sir Thomas Picton, whose cavalry regiment was due to embark for Ostend on 11 June. Picton, who had a sense of foreboding – justified as it turned out, as he was killed at Waterloo – and expected casualties among his staff, was happy to take Gronow as a supernumerary. All the captain needed was the price of two good horses at Tattershalls and the services of a groom, but this was way beyond Gronow's means, or so it seemed. However, having borrowed a cool £200 – perhaps £9,000 in today's money – from indulgent friends at Cox & Greenwood's, the army supply agents, Gronow played blackjack at 'a gambling house on St James' Square' and with admirable self-restraint, emerged with the requisite £600. Discreetly omitted from his published memoirs but later recalled at a dinner party in France, was that Gronow smuggled two young ladies as well-bred as his horses on to the boat at Ramsgate. Word had got around Almack's that the Duchess of Richmond was holding a rather special ball and the unidentified pair, almost certainly without the approval of their mothers, were resolved to attend this supremely attractive marriage market.

Wellington had given a 'Grand Rout' himself on 8 June, with four invitations to each regiment. His officers knew that proficiency in dancing was a prerequisite for promotion in the eyes of the Duke. One lucky young subaltern loudly told envious colleagues that 'Wellington has sent me a ball ticket', just as his supreme commander rode by. 'At least call me Mr Wellington', said Lord

Wellington, looking back in mock disapproval. As quick as a flash the young man, sensing the opportunity for repartee, replied: 'My Lord, we do not speak of Mr Caesar or Mr Alexander, so why should I speak of Mr Wellington?'

The Duchess was led into supper at the Duke's Rout by the Prince of Orange. Her husband had just been told he might take charge of the Brussels reserve army. This was an empty gesture without rank or pay since Wellington had very few reserves worthy of the name, and an extremely low opinion of Richmond's military capabilities. But it gave the Duchess an excuse for presenting her forthcoming ball scheduled for 15 June as a quasi-government occasion. She was proving as obdurate an opponent for Wellington as he expected Napoleon to be. Brussels was little more than an armed camp and only someone as blinkered and domineering as the Duchess would have challenged the commander-in-chief or as she called him, the Padrone, on virtually the eve of battle.

A bust of Charlotte, Duchess of Richmond, by Joseph Nollekens. They never met but Nollekins captured her domineering demeanour perfectly

'My dear Duke', said she to Wellington, 'may I give my ball?' 'If you say, "Duchess, don't give your ball," it is quite sufficient. I ask no reasons.'

Wellington, aware that his own next ball was still in the calendar for 21 June, and that whatever he said would be turned into a dispatch for Bonaparte's breakfast table in a matter of days, was completely trapped. He gave his only possible answer.

'Duchess, you may give your ball with the greatest safety, without fear of interruption.'

That same night la Bédoyère was also to be found in Brussels, where sympathisers of Napoleon provided him with a base and stabled his horse. He found the entrances to Wellington's ball too well guarded but had a conversation with several excited young officers as they left to rejoin their regiments. Thanks to the ubiquitous Miss Plunkett, Charles spoke almost fluent English, albeit with a slight accent, and could easily pass as a loyal member of Wellington's cosmopolitan force. For five days he toured the country, visiting dozens of towns and villages where the troops were billeted.

Napoleon's uniforms, telescopes, maps and carriages had already been made ready for his departure. On 12 June, while the Duchess was opportunistically borrowing the British Embassy plate for the use of her guests at supper during her own forthcoming ball, the Emperor left Paris to join Marshal Ney and the 125,000-strong Army of the North at Avesnes. The following evening he received a detailed report from la Bédoyère on the size and disposition of the Anglo-Dutch army. He was able to tell Napoleon that Wellington did not expect a French invasion for some time, if indeed at all, and that both his and the Prussian troops remained widely dispersed. Based on his assessment, Bonaparte brought his army close to the frontier and at dawn on 15 June was poised to seize the bridges at Charleroi.

Later that day he sent la Bédoyère back into the Netherlands on an even bolder spying mission. Just after sunset, ostensibly acting on orders from Lieutenant-General Henry Paget, Lord Uxbridge, Charles rode into Strijtem. This tranquil Flemish village some twenty kilometres west of Brussels had been occupied by a British artillery troop for the previous six weeks.

'He was dressed as our hussars usually were when riding about the country – blue frock, scarlet waistcoat laced with gold, pantaloons, and a forage cap of the 7th Hussars. He was mounted on a smart pony, with plain saddle and bridge, was without sword and sash, and carried a small whip, in short his costume and monture [the way he sat on a horse] were correct in every particular. Moreover, he aped to the very life that "devil-may-care" nonchalant air so frequently characterising our young men of fashion'.

So wrote 22-year-old Captain Alexander Cavalié Mercer in his Waterloo Journal, recalling how the spy discovered how many men and horses were quartered in the village, whose troop they belonged to, and where and in what numbers the remainder of the troop could be found. Charles rode off having audaciously castigated the innkeeper and mayor in fluent French for not having room for another imaginary 200 horses. It was later discovered of course that no officer had been sent by Lord Uxbridge on any such activity. Mercer concluded with grudging admiration: 'Our friend deserved to escape, for he was a bold and clever fellow'. As acting commander 'G Troop' Royal Artillery, Mercer felt he had no option but to remain at his post that evening, while some of his fellow officers rode into Brussels to attend the Duchess of Richmond's Ball. La Bédoyère, having tested his latest disguise to his complete satisfaction, was on his way there, too.

And so was Captain Gronow, pledged to deliver his two fair charges to the Duchess, who needed extra young ladies to make the ball more appealing to the young officers on her invitation list. He managed to keep them and the lascivious 57-year-old General Picton apart – the general was seen at Ostend chatting up a pretty hotel waitress in perfect French – by taking a barge to Ghent and post haste a coach straight on to Brussels. Picton and his staff travelled more leisurely the whole way by road and arrived at 4 p.m. on 15 June, to find there was no room at the inn, any inn. Gronow however knew the manager of the Hotel d'Angleterre on the rue de la Madeleine and as if by a miracle, three rooms were produced, ingratiating him still further with the general.

The Duchess's society intelligence service was at fever pitch, and within the hour, courtesy of the British Ambassador's running footman, an invitation to the ball duly arrived for General Picton. Gronow intercepted it. He was not so foolish as to expect his own invitation from the Duchess as a reward for his efforts, since she was such a snob. But if he was going to be even a fringe guest at the ball, partaking of its unlimited free alcohol, he needed to make sure that Picton did not turn up. Then Gronow, wondering how he could bluff his way into the 'Wash-House', had a stroke of luck. The Duchess commandeered some ordinary ranks from the Welsh foot guards to help with security and some heavy lifting in the ballroom. They included a huge 6ft. 7in., unusually literate Welsh private from Gronow's own regiment: Gareth Hughes, whose father was a chapel minister. Hughes turned a Nelson eye to a fellow Welshman with a borrowed ticket despite being under strict orders from the Duchess to scrutinise the ball invitations vigorously at the front door. They had been prepared at a small print shop owned by her landlord, Michel-Jean Simons. The Duchess was far too determined to beat down his price to notice when one of the blank invitations deliberately went astray. It ended up in the hands of the enemy. This was the means by which Charles de la Bédoyère, complete with gold-embossed invitation card, became for the evening a convincing man for all seasons, a certain Colonel Durngler: British but not British, Dutch but not Dutch, possibly Belgian French but certainly not loyal to the Union Jack.

Michel-Jean Simons, a jack of all trades, ran a print shop as well as a coach-making business and printed the invitations for the Duchess of Richmond's Ball

Definitely absent from Charlotte's guest list was Sir Neil Campbell, desperately trying to save his reputation and career. He exercised his right to purchase a commission in his old regiment, the 54th Foot, dropping down to the rank of major in the process, and had arrived that very day after sailing from Ramsgate to Ostend on the humble mail packet boat. His fellow traveller by chance was Charlotte Ann Waldie, a 26-year-old banker's daughter with a burning ambition to become a writer. The charming Major Campbell proved able to arrange a room for her in Brussels at the Hotel de Flandre. At 10 p.m. that night, just as a traffic jam of coaches built up in the streets around the 'Wash-House', signalling the start of the ball, Charlotte heard a tap on her bedroom door. Major Campbell, 'magnificent in a full dress uniform, covered with crosses, clasps, orders and medals, the white outline of a scar beneath the left eye', asked to be admitted. He said he had 'dined' (he meant 'lunched' in modern terms) with Wellington and had alarming news. Charlotte agonised… for a second. How could she refuse such a 'splendid beau' but 'at such a late hour, alone in her bedroom of all places, what would they have thought in England?' Sir Neil had brought with him a decanter of whisky. Charlotte said she rang the bell and ordered tea. If so, twenty-four hour room service, a comparatively modern phenomenon, made its first recorded appearance a century earlier. According to her version, after an hour's conversation that was 'much to our mutual satisfaction, Sir Neil Campbell went away'. However, whatever took place that evening, Charlotte did not get much sleep. At 2.30 a.m. she was roused by her brother John to say a tearful farewell to an old family friend, Major Richard Llewellyn of the 28th Foot, whose horse was eager to be off to war, whinnying and pawing the cobbles in the courtyard below.

Campbell would have no chance of glory at Waterloo. The 54th Foot were held in reserve, protecting the route to the Channel ports, and received not so much as a medal. Campbell left the army and returned to the diplomatic service, where, in desperation and despite the pleas of his family, in 1826 he accepted the poisoned chalice of the governorship of Sierra Leone. The following August he died of a tropical fever in 'that pestilential climate', the third of four successive governors to survive for less than a year.

In June 1815, friend and foe alike wanted to know: would Wellington, the star of Brussel's social firmament, go to the Duchess's ball? The eight months pregnant Caroline Capel, already resigned to being an absentee, said 'nobody can guess Lord Wellington's intentions and… in the meantime he amuses himself with humbugging the ladies, particularly the Duchess of Richmond'. Alarming reports were coming in that the French were on the move. At 11.30 p.m. the Duke was still closeted with Colonel Friedrich Karl von Müffling, the Prussian liaison officer, who had a dispatch for Field Marshal Gebhard von Blücher half prepared; all he had to do was fill in the names and map references of the rendezvous. Von Müffling looked immaculate, in full dress uniform medals up, although curiously, he had no actual invitation to the 'Wash-House'. Wellington was half dressed and hurried in, with a rolled map under his arm, wearing his scarlet dressing-gown and slippers. 'The numerous friends of Napoleon who are here, will be tempted to raise their heads', he told von Müffling. 'The well-disposed must be tranquillised. Let us therefore go, all the same, to the Duchess of Richmond's Ball.'

The Duchess had been almost prostrate with anxiety at the continued absence of her most important guest. It was left to her 17-year-old daughter Lady Georgiana to establish the facts. Wellington had known 'dearest Georgy' since her tenth birthday. The moment he arrived, just before midnight, she left the dance floor in the middle of a waltz and asked him point-blank about the rumours. The Duke said gravely, 'They are all true. We are off tomorrow'. The news spread through the assembled officers like wildfire.

Meanwhile for Major-General Baron Jan-Viktor de Constant-Rebecque, chief of staff to the Prince of Orange, who had also gone to Brussels for the ball, the Duke's orders earlier in the day had become a serious problem. They left a key crossroads, Les Quatre Bras, only lightly guarded, and by troops short of ammunition. Wellington had no idea that the French had driven out the advance guard of the Prussians and were only 35 kilometres from Brussels. Fortunately Constant-Rebecque, almost alone of Wellington's commanders, had known him long enough and had the self-confidence to countermand his instructions.

At 10.30 p.m. he sent the Duke a note on his fastest rider, Lieutenant Henry Webster of the 9th Light Dragoons. He did not have an invitation to the ball and was bored beyond belief, lounging outside the Hotel de Miroir at Brain-le-Comte. Constant-Rebecque told him: 'There's a horse saddled-up outside and another in readiness halfway: gallop every metre! Do not take no for an answer, insist on seeing the Prince at once!' On a paved road, Webster completed the 30 kilometres in two hours. He leapt off his second mount at half past midnight, hoping to find the prince in his headquarters on the rue de Brabant. Learning that he was already at the ball, Webster rode into the Grand' Place but such was the crush of carriages, could go no further on horseback.

He ran the rest of the way to the rue de la Blanchisserie, only to be asked to wait. 'The Duchess has just given orders for the band to go upstairs and the guests are just about to rise', he was told, 'If you were to burst in suddenly, it might alarm the ladies'. Once again engaging the enemy was playing second fiddle to the ball.

Webster hid behind a folding scullery door and watched as the man he was desperate to see, the Prince of Orange, walked to the foot of the stairs arm in arm with the Duchess, following by the Duke and Lady Charlotte Greville. Webster sidled up behind them and thrust his dispatch under the Prince's nose. Recognising Webster, the prince signalled him to stay put, started up the stairs, and handed the note to the Duke, who thrust it into his coat pocket. As the VIP party took their seats for supper, Wellington read the message, walked back downstairs and told Webster to summon the Prince's coach and four. Some furious whispering ensued, whereupon the Prince asked to be excused. It later transpired that Wellington had no fresh orders but had strongly suggested he should return to Braine-le-Comte immediately. The Duchess sat fuming about the empty place thereby created next to her at the dining table but the Duke defused the atmosphere by reaching into his pocket. To general applause, he presented Lady Georgiana with a miniature of himself, painted by a Belgian artist since his arrival in Brussels.

Lady Georgiana Lennox, daughter of the Duchess of Richmond, was always the Duke of Wellington's favourite. During supper at the ball Wellington presented her with a miniature of himself produced by Simon Rochard, a Brussels artist

Henry Webster, the son of Lady Holland by her late and unlamented husband, Sir Godfrey Webster, would come through the next few days' action unscathed. The fame he enjoyed, the first to bring news to Wellington at the ball of the full extent of the French advance, proved all too fleeting. Henry broke off his engagement to a local beauty, Elisabeth de Hamm, blaming 'orders' from his mother for leaving her 'in the lurch in hysterics'. The disapproving ladies of the Belgian nobility did not wield the power of Almack's patronesses but they still made Webster virtually a social outcast. The Hereditary Prince of Orange dropped him as his aide-de-camp and he was forced to return to England with

Lieutenant Henry Webster, who rode 30 kilometres in two hours to bring Wellington vital news of the advancing French. Soon afterwards Webster jilted his fiancée, a member of a leading Brussels family, and blighted his army career despite his newfound fame

his tail between his legs. In 1847 Webster would follow his father in committing suicide, cutting his throat in gruesome fashion with a penknife.

After Webster's arrival on the night of the ball, Wellington told General Hill, the commander of II Corps, to depart immediately. To his aide Captain Mackworth, without a ball partner, this was something of a relief:

'In our ball costumes, brilliant with gold lace and embroidery, exulting that our long tiresome days of inactivity were at an end, and... [realising] we were on the point of meeting this celebrated lou-garou [werewolf] Bonaparte, so long our anxious wish'.

(previous page) The Duchess of Richmond's Ball by Robert Hillingford, who depicted a much grander venue than the converted coach house. Lieutenant Webster is shown delivering to Wellington his warning about the French advance but in reality this took place elsewhere in the house, at the foot of the stairs as the VIP party went up for supper

Duke Friedrich-Wilhelm von Braunschweig-Luneberg, also in the ballroom, needed no second telling. Forgetting that he had the latest Prince de Ligne, 10-year-old Eugene Lamoral, sitting on his knee, he sprang to his feet and dropped the child heavily on the floor. As Eugene's mother, countess Louise d'Oultremont, picked up him up rather indignantly, Friedrich, deathly pale, apologised profusely and took his leave. On the way out he told Lady Georgiana that his Brunswickers would 'fight with honour'. A day later he would be dead.

(opposite & below) John Everitt Millais's romantic interpretation of the Black Brunswicker's reluctant departure from the Duchess of Richmond's Ball. Duke Friedrich-Wilhelm von Braunschweig-Luneberg dressed his Brunswickers in black in mourning at the loss of his duchy during the Napoleonic wars. The day after the ball, he died from injuries received during the Battle of Quatre Bras

Because of the accident that had befallen William Lennox, his place as ADC to Major-General Peregrine Maitland was taken by 17-year-old James the Lord Hay, eldest son of the Earl of Errol. Hay had no choice but to follow his commanding officer out of the building. This handsome ensign in the first regiment of Guards, immaculately turned out in full dress uniform, with silk hose and silver-buckled shoes, was unashamedly lusted after. 'He's very poor I hear', said one young lady ruefully, 'but very good looking!' The 'dashing, merry youth' had also become something of a Brussels celebrity. Several times a week, riding his superb thoroughbred mare Muzzy, he leapt over the railings into the royal park until, fruitlessly chased by the keepers, he would leap out again. One day, aided by a dozen gendarmes, they set a trap for him but left a huge, seemingly impossible barrier unguarded, which Hay triumphantly cleared on Muzzy and escaped. Only when the city mayor complained to Wellington, did Hay regretfully end his equine feats. At the ball, 'full of military ardour…and of all the honours he was to gain', his parting promise to his tearful sweetheart, Lady Maria Capel, was that if he should fall in the first action, Muzzy would be hers to keep. Hay had only a few hours left to live.

James, Lord Hay, unashamedly lusted after by the ladies of Brussels. 'Full of military ardour', the day after the ball he was shot dead during the Battle of Quatre Bras

As the tide of departing officers became a flood, the Duchess became quite hysterical. Said Mackworth, 'In vain did the *afflicted* Duchess of Richmond, placing herself at the entrance to the ballroom, pray and entreat that we would not "go before supper" [the separate buffet destined for the hoi polloi]; that we would wait "one hour more"; and "not spoil her ball". It was no use, added Mackworth, being 'ungentle hard-hearted cavaliers, we resisted all [entreaties] and departed'. No doubt Charlotte would have been content to receive Napoleon himself as an honoured guest, so long as his Imperial Guard had the good manners to wait outside. She did not notice 'Colonel Durngler', in all the bustle and confusion, choosing this opportune moment to disappear.

Perhaps fortunately for the Duchess, Wellington was too distracted to appreciate her antics. Lady Jane Dalrymple-Hamilton said she 'had never seen him have such an expression of care and anxiety on his countenance. I sat next to him on a sofa for a long time but his mind seemed quite pre-occupied and, although he spoke to me in the kindest manner possible, yet frequently in the middle of a sentence he stopped abruptly and called to some officer, giving him directions'.

The Duchess, regarding her ball as ruined, was probably not far short of suicidal. Her daughter Jane was much more sensitive to the inevitable change of mood.

'I know I was in a state of wild delight. The scene itself was so stirring and the company so brilliant', she wrote later. 'On reaching the ballroom after supper, I was scanning my tablets, filled from top to bottom with the names of the partners... when, on raising my eyes, I became aware of the great preponderance of ladies in the room... The enigma was soon solved. Without fuss or parade, or tender adieux, the officers, anxious not to alarm the ladies, had quietly stolen out... before we had time to guess the nature of the news'.

(previous page) Henry O'Neil's work, 'Before Waterloo', showed how guests at the Duchess of Richmond's Ball spread out from the ballroom. However very few of Wellington's officers took formal leave of their partners, preferring to steal away quietly and avoid a painful farewell

A few of the officers sensed the momentous nature of the occasion, even though the ball was never completed and took place not on the eve of Waterloo but of the Battle of Quatre Bras, two days earlier. Captains Standish O'Grady and William Verner of the 7th Hussars, who brought their dress uniforms with them from a distant outpost and changed at the Hotel de la Reine du Suede, were just arriving at the 'Wash-House' when they met one of Wellington's ADCs, Lieutenant George Lennox, in the courtyard at 1.30 a.m. He told them the ball was effectively over and he had summoned the Duke's coach. Verner turned to O'Grady and said, 'Let's go into the ballroom, at least to say we were there'. They found it 'in the greatest confusion and… The officers were hurrying away as fast as possible.' Even so, what the Duchess with incredible humbug and hypocrisy later called some 'energetic and heartless young ladies', still wanted to waltz. No doubt they included Captain Gronow's young imports, who were left to find their own way back to England. With women now outnumbering their male counterparts by ten to one, Lord Uxbridge decided it was time to bring the entertainment to a close. He came to the ballroom door and said, 'You gentlemen who have engaged partners had better finish your dance and get to your quarters'. The band, stopping in mid-bar, pre-empted even that.

Wellington saw the general exodus and turned to Richmond, saying, "It's time for me to go to bed likewise'. Almost as an afterthought, he asked his host if he had a good map in his study-bedroom, directly opposite the ballroom. Behind its closed door, Wellington spread out his map on the bed. 'Bonaparte has humbugged me by God', he said, 'he has gained twenty-four hours march on me'. With Richmond at his shoulder, Wellington said, 'we shall not stop him there', indicating Quatre Bras, 'and if so, I must fight him here', placing his thumbnail on a defensive position just south of Waterloo. Bidding Richmond 'adieu', he left the house by a side door.

Chapter Eight

A Lunchtime Affair!

ONLY ONE officer, turning Wellington's orders into formal dispatches long into the night, remained in the rue de la Blanchisserie: Colonel Sir William De Lancey. Born in New York, he was the only son of the clerk of the county of Albany and a vicar's daughter in what was still the little Apple. As ill-timed supporters of King George III, all their property was confiscated by the US administration. They left to start a new life in England. De Lancey distinguished himself as a man who could get things done and was at Wellington's side for much of the Peninsula campaign. When peace came in 1814 and large parts of the army were disbanded, he kept his rank and was posted to Edinburgh. Within a matter of weeks he embarked on a whirlwind romance with Magdalene, the beautiful daughter of Sir James Hall of Dunglas, 4th Baronet, a wealthy Scottish landowner. The first night of their blissful honeymoon coincided with Wellington's arrival in Brussels. Four days later a messenger reached Scotland bearing a handwritten note from the Duke, offering De Lancey the post of Deputy Quarter-Master General. With decided lack of enthusiasm, De Lancey agreed to serve. He arrived in Brussels on 25 May, followed by Magdalene on 8 June. They rented a set of rooms on the fourth floor of a house belonging to the comte de Lannoy and overlooking the park.

Born in New York, Sir William De Lancey fought with Wellington throughout the entire Peninsula campaign. His whirlwind romance with Magdalene Hall ended with a summons from Wellington in 1815 but the new Lady De Lancey joined him in Brussels and would soon find herself a widow

Lady de Lancey, who had led a sheltered life in Scotland, immediately upset convention by eschewing the relentless round of balls and parties altogether. 'I wasted no time in visiting or going to Balls, which I did not care for,' she said simply. 'I never went out, except for an hour or two to walk with Sir William'. Even those walks were deliberately timed to coincide with the dinner period of 3.p.m., so Magdalene saw hardly anyone, except a few intimate friends her husband from time to time brought home to dinner. William was not at all stretched in his role until just before Waterloo, and according to Magdalene 'only went to the office for about an hour every day'. It is not hard to deduce that the newly wedded lovers spent a great deal of time at home in bed. Magdalene's 'life [was] gliding on, like a gay dream'. On 15 June, that dream was shattered for ever.

William had accepted an invitation to dine out for once, with the Spanish chargé d'affaires. At 7 p.m. he was summoned back, galloping furiously past Magdalene, who happened to be looking out of the window, to the Duke's headquarters a few doors away. He was in such a rush he ran inside leaving his horse, untethered and bewildered, in the middle of the street. At 9 p.m. he returned home just long enough to tell Magdalene war was imminent and that she should pack her belongings to leave for Antwerp, with other British residents, by coach arranged to depart at 6.a.m the following day. He was home again briefly just after midnight but fortified by strong green team brewed by his wife, he soon returned to Wellington's side.

Magdalene and William received invitations for the Duchess of Richmond's ball but as usual had no intention of attending. De Lancey arrived at the ball in its final hour only at Wellington's insistence, to write out yet more troop orders. He was present in Richmond's study when the Duke acknowledged that Napoleon, almost literally, had stolen a march on him. But it took more than a setback to disturb Wellington's composure for long. When De Lancey went back to see him with some queries, just after 2 a.m., the Duke's staff told him Wellington was already sound asleep and had left strict instructions not to be disturbed. De Lancey suspected however that Lady Webster, seated beside Wellington at supper, had not returned to her own residence and was warming his bed.

Some of the guests, including Colonel Sir William Ponsonby, were beginning to regret going to the ball and having to mobilise with little or no sleep. 'I am quite knocked up', he told a subordinate. Others were blundering about the countryside, their troops having moved complete with baggage on Wellington's orders while they danced. Some had no option but to fight in their dress uniforms. Lieutenant Basil Jackson of the Royal Staff Corps, who carried many such dispatches that night, 'fell in with several officers of rank making for their troops'. 'Knowing all the arrangements for the army generally,' he boasted, 'I was able to tell them what roads to take in order to intercept their divisions'. At the ball, he had been a mine of useful information to a very interested Colonel Durngler, too.

Later on the morning of 16 June, la Bédoyère, no doubt feeling extremely pleased with himself, eventually found a way around the allied forces threatened at the pivotal crossroads of Quatre Bras and returned to the French lines. But perhaps because Napoleon had spent the night far behind the front, for several critical hours la Bédoyère seems to have lost touch with the Emperor. Left to his own devices, he became directly responsible for the contradiction in orders that saved the Prussians from complete disaster at Ligny, cost his commander-in-chief victory at Quatre Bras and would influence the outcome of Waterloo itself. Jean-Baptiste Droué, comte d'Erlon, at one point within four kilometres of Quatre Bras while it was still thinly defended, spent the whole day leading his force of 20,000 men and 46 pieces of artillery between two battlefields separated by just nine kilometres, without taking part in either. As Marshal Ney harshly described it, they 'idly paraded during the whole of the battle from the right to the left, and the left to the right, without firing a shot'.

Napoleon's main forces arrived at the pivotal crossroads of Quatre Bras too late to prevent Wellington's retreat to prepared positions just south of the village of Waterloo

At about 4.30 p.m. one of d'Erlon's divisions was intercepted by la Bédoyère on the Brussels road. He carried with him what became known as the famous, or infamous, note in pencil, ordering d'Erlon's entire corps to change direction and march on the Prussians at Ligny. D'Erlon's senior officers could hear the sound of cannon fire up ahead and did not give in easily; but Charles eventually convinced them that the order came directly from the Emperor himself. To make sure it would not be countermanded, la Bédoyère then galloped after d'Erlon, who was with the rest of his column, about two kilometres away. On catching up with d'Erlon, who knew Charles well from previous campaigns, he showed him the note and presented the count with a fait accompli, telling him that his corps had already started to move in the direction of Ligny. Since neither Napoleon nor his generals gave any such order, the only credible explanation is that la Bédoyère, with extraordinary hubris, believing he was doing the right thing based on what he had learned of the latest allied troop movements at the Duchess of Richmond's Ball, wrote the note himself.

Wellington's battalions retreated in good order to his pre-determined position on the ridge before Waterloo, with De Lancey personally driving in stakes along the whole front, marking the exact places where the allied regiments were to be deployed. However, la Bédoyère's vivid account that night of what took place at the ball in Brussels can only have reinforced Bonaparte's belief that Wellington's army, irrespective of its position, was there for the taking. The generals who had faced him in the Peninsula War knew better, and at a breakfast conference with the Emperor the following morning Marshal Soult in particular suggested he could not rely on being able to break what became known as 'the thin red line'. Napoleon replied, 'Just because you've been beaten by Wellington, you have to consider him a good general. I say he's a bad general and the English make poor troops. It will be a lunchtime affair!' On Sunday, 18 June 1815, sunrise occurred at 3.48 a.m. Napoleon's general order for the attack was not written until 11 a.m. Those lost hours were enough to ensure that Wellington's huge gamble came off, the arrival of the Prussians in sufficient numbers to alter the outcome of the battle.

Even then, at 7 p.m. la Bédoyère was to play out another role that helped to turn defeat into a complete disaster. Perhaps a third of Napoleon's force had been detached under General Grouchy to shadow the Prussians. They received messages recalling them far too late. In an effort to revive the morale of his weary men, Bonaparte sent la Bédoyère riding along the front to put out what was a naked lie, that the guns they could hear belonged to Grouchy, attacking the Prussian rear. However the shells were falling not on the Prussians but on the French lines, who assumed that Grouchy had changed sides. After the failure of Napoleon's last throw of the dice, a disorganised advance by only part of his Imperial Guard, his army collapsed into a general rout. La Bédoyère, distraught at the panic his eloquence had created, wanted to die sword in hand on the battlefield and had to be dragged away to safety before night fell.

Captain Gronow began the momentous day in the cavalry and ended it a foot soldier. Picton could not find a role for him and sent him back to his own regiment.

'Taking his advice, I rode off to where the Guards were stationed; the officers—amongst whom I remember Colonel Thomas and Brigade-Major Miller—expressed their astonishment and amazement on seeing me, and exclaimed, "What the deuce brought you here? Why are you not with your battalion in London? Get off your horse, and explain how you came here!"

'Things were beginning to look a little awkward, when Gunthorpe, the adjutant, a great friend of mine, took my part and said, "As he is here, let us make the most of him; there's plenty of work for everyone. Come, Gronow, you shall go with Captain Clements and a detachment to the village of Waterloo, to take charge of the French prisoners." I said, "What the deuce shall I do with my horse?" Upon which Captain Stopford, aide-de-camp to Sir John Byng, volunteered to buy him. Having once more become a foot soldier, I started according to orders, and arrived at Waterloo.'

Thus it came about that at around 7.p.m., against Wellington's instructions, the Welsh foot guards, cold and hungry, after a day under artillery fire, did not wait to receive the front ranks of the Imperial Guard but fell on them ferociously in hand-to-hand combat. Gronow saw the giant Hughes, fresh from the gate at the Duchess's ball, and usually more at home with a prayer book, 'run through with his bayonet, and knock down with the butt end of his firelock, I should think a dozen at least of his opponents'. Many were without breastplates, a shortage of equipment Napoleon had dismissed as of no consequence on 3 June. In any event, however, British regiments had been taught to aim low and make every shot count. According to Gronow, Lieutenant-Colonel Sir Charles Belson, commander of the 28th Foot, told his men, 'be sure to fire at these Frenchies' legs and spoil their dancing'.

Another eye witness of Waterloo was the Duke of Richmond who, foolish as ever, not only rode out from Brussels to watch the battle but took his seriously injured son with him. William felt obliged to present himself for duty with Maitland, who took one look at his bandaged right eye, his maimed right arm in a sling and his deathly grey pallor, and said he was in no condition to be an efficient ADC. Lord William then joined his father, who had attached himself to Wellington's headquarters. When Wellington saw them, in the midst of the fighting, he told William, 'You should be in bed', and turned with fury to Richmond and said, 'You have no business here'. Richmond failed to take the hint but rode about the field, making casual conversation with officers he knew, giving (usually bad) advice and behaving as though he had an official role on active service. Finally in mid-afternoon, with the battle still in the balance, and the ground strewn with the slain, Wellington lost patience and gave them a direct order to return to Brussels.

The three days of fighting went badly for several at the ball. The Duke von Braunschweig, rallying his men at Quatre Bras, was killed by a musket ball that penetrated his lungs and liver. On the same afternoon Lord Hay was shot dead, hit in the head by a bullet fired by a French cavalry skirmisher. Lady Maria Capel never did get his horse. The 'fatigued' Sir William Ponsonby, foolishly and needlessly charging the French cavalry at Waterloo, was lanced to death.

The Duke of Richmond came out from Brussels with his injured son William to watch the Battle of Waterloo and acted as though he had an official position. Wellington told him, 'You have no business here,' and eventually ordered them to leave

Lieutenant-Colonel Sir Alexander Gordon, one of Wellington's ADCs, was struck high on the right thigh by grapeshot. His right leg had to be amputated and he died from loss of blood. William De Lancey, riding beside Wellington, was fatally injured by a cannon ball bouncing along *en ricochet*. It glanced off without breaking his skin or even damaging his coat, but the sheer momentum separated eight of the ribs on his left side from his back. One rib was broken in fourteen places and a surgeon found that part of it had entered a lung. De Lancey lingered on for ten days in a tiny abandoned cottage at nearby Mont St Jean, his bed little more than a broken frame attached to the wall. He was devotedly

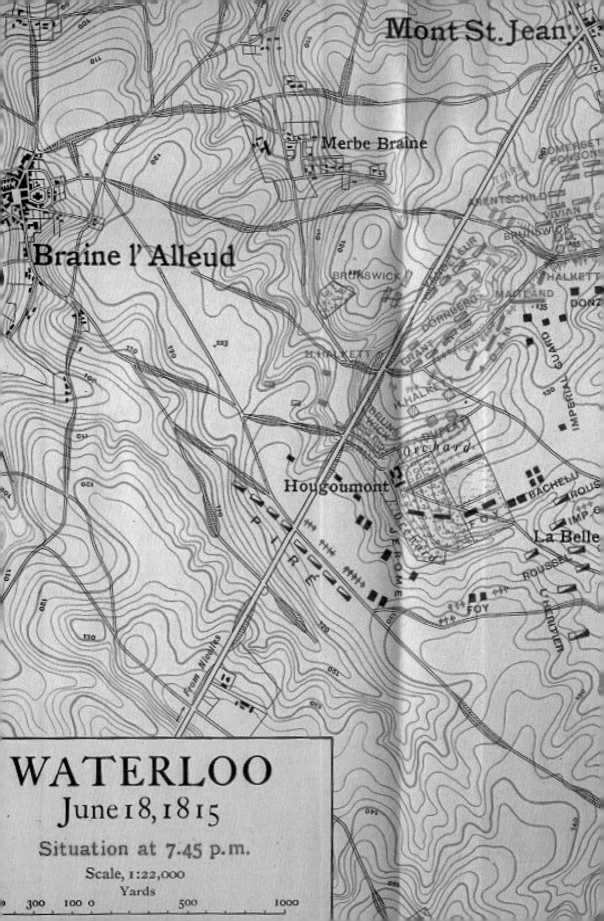

Mont St. Jean

Merbe Braine

Braine l'Alleud

BRUNSWICK

Hougoumont

Orchard

La Belle

WATERLOO
June 18, 1815

Situation at 7.45 p.m.

Scale, 1:22,000

Yards

300 100 0   500   1000

nt St. Jean Farm

La Haye Sainte

MARCOGNET

VACQUINOT

SUBERVIE

DOMON

IMPERIAL
GUARD

Plancenoit

Rossomme

Papelotte

La Haie

Smohain

Frischermont

(previous page) The critical moment at Waterloo when with the Prussians already playing a major role in the battle, Napoleon sends part of his Imperial Guard to attack the Anglo-Dutch line

nursed by Magdalene, from time to time snatching a few moments' sleep in the hovel's solitary wooden chair, having made the perilous journey out to find him. Despite this traumatic experience, the widowed Magdalene was nothing if not resilient. In March 1817 she married another army officer, Captain Henry Harvey. Her letters to him during their courtship contained passages in code, thought to be explicit sexual references. They had three children but in 1822 Magdalene, aged 29, died from complications following the birth of the third.

In contrast to his staff, Wellington seemed to enjoy a charmed life during the three days of fighting. Colonel Charles Best saw him sitting on the edge of a ditch writing a troop order when a cannon ball hit the ground so close, it covered him with earth. Wellington glanced across to the new hole in the ground, shook off the earth, and continued writing his order as though it was a Sunday afternoon in the park.

The Duke of Wellington seemed to have a charmed life at the Battle of Waterloo. Many of his commanders, and most of his staff officers, were either killed or seriously injured

Within days of the fighting, before all the wounded casualties had been removed from the battlefield, the village of Waterloo had a macabre market for souvenirs

After the battle, most social life in Brussels ceased, out of practicality rather than respect, as almost every able-bodied man was pursuing the French. The Duke's ball was cancelled: the carnage had left him with no stomach for celebration. Richmond, unperturbed, amused himself by escorting titled British ladies to Waterloo, whose village was already the centre of a frenetic trade in macabre souvenirs. At the end of June, Wellington set out for France on horseback but accompanied by all the comforts of home. His cook, James Thornton, recalled a procession of five splendid carriages, one for the Duke, one for the plate, one for the kitchen furniture, one for the baggage, and finally the Duke's chaise and pair.

Chapter Nine

Thirteen at Dinner

THE BATTLE LOST, La Bédoyère left his morose and defeated Emperor behind in his coach. Probably on his instructions, he rode ahead furiously to Paris, attempting to rally support for Napoleon by claiming France had beaten the allies at Waterloo. Charles was increasingly losing touch with reality. When he harangued the Chamber of Deputies, Marshal Massena publicly rebuked him: 'Young man, you forget who you are!' It was left to Marshal Ney calmly to admit the truth and Napoleon abdicated for a second time.

The remnants of the French Army of the North fell back, pursued and harried by the Prussians. Charles went for dinner at the château du Malmaison just outside Paris, invited by his strongest supporter and rumoured lover, Napoleon's sister-in-law and step-daughter, Queen Hortense of the Netherlands. With the Prussians less than eight kilometres from the capital, the gloomy atmosphere was made gloomier by the discovery that there were thirteen at table. According to superstition, observed Queen Hortense, one of their number would die within a year. La Bédoyère said sadly, 'In all probability Your Majesty's prediction will come true in me: the Bourbons will never forgive the part I played in joining the Emperor on his return from Elba.' It was the time of the White Terror, when the Royalists demanded their pound of flesh from the Bonapartists, citing a dozen officers for treason, including Ney and Charles, who for a while made himself scarce in the Loire valley.

(opposite) Hortense de Beauharnais, Queen of the Netherlands, Napoleon's stepdaughter, was a fervent supporter of Charles de la Bédoyère. Hortense persuaded her long-term lover, the comte de Flahaut, to issue la Bédoyère with a passport to leave France for the United States but he was arrested before he could make use of it

A charcoal sketch of Charles de la Bedoyere by Hortense de Beauharnais from early 1815, when it is likely they were lovers. This was his only triumph over Wellington. During his time in Paris the Duke was led on by Hortense for political advantage but for once had to settle for a racy picture of her on his bedroom wall

With Talleyrand still clinging to office, la Bédoyère obtained a false passport to emigrate to the United States, helped by the prime minister's natural son, his own distant cousin, Charles du Flahaut. However, on 2 August 1815 he foolishly returned to Paris to spend a last night with his wife and baby son. The French police had staked out his house and in the morning, Charles was arrested. Georgine wrote to the Duke of Wellington on 11 and 13 August asking him to approach Louis XVIII with a request for clemency. They fell on deaf ears. La Bédoyère did not help himself with the arrogant assertion made during his initial interrogation by Lieutenant Étienne Martin of the Paris prefecture, solemnly recorded by Leoncé Grasilier, that he had hoodwinked the British Army by attending the Duchess of Richmond's ball.

On 14 August Charles went on trial, a lengthy judicial process that included a spectacular fainting fit by a publicity-seeking French actress, all avidly followed by the readers of the *London Times*. In a last desperate and unavailing appeal, Georgine, already clad in mourning black, flung herself at Louis's feet as he returned by coach to the Tuileries. He said sadly, 'Madame, never has a refusal cost me so much'. She would be a widow for 55 years. On the evening of 19 August, la Bédoyère was taken in front of a firing squad outside the École Militaire near the Champ du Mars. With typical élan, scorning a blindfold, he gave the command to fire himself. '*Sur tout, ne me manquez pas!*' ('Above all, don't miss!') were his final words.

La Bédoyère was found guilty of treason and executed in Paris by firing squad. He took command of the detail himself with typical élan and ordered them to shoot straight

For Britain's conquering hero, life resumed its normal pattern, except that not content with defeating Napoleon on the battlefield, Wellington had to beat him in bed as well. His latest conquest was another of Napoleon's former lovers, the actress known as 'Mademoiselle Georges', Marguerite-Josephine Weimer, daughter of a German musician. Not long afterwards, audaciously asked by a fellow guest at a dinner party to compare the sexual prowess of the two immortals, Marguerite-Josephine replied, 'the Duke was by far the more vigorous'. Napoleon was undoubtedly the more generous, once pushing 40,000 francs down her cleavage (as historian Andrew Roberts quipped, presumably in notes). Madame de Staële, who got to know the parsimonious Wellington well in her twilight years, sagely observed that 'Never has God created a great man with less expenditure… he has "*pas de coeur pour l'amour*" ("no heart for true love")'.

Marguerite-Josephine Weimer, known as Mademoiselle Georges, was the mistress of both Napoleon and the Duke of Wellington. Asked to compare their sexual prowess, she said that Wellington was by far the more vigorous

With Brussels once again a backwater, the festivities and the mistresses moved to Paris. Literally so on 1 August, when the Duke gave the grandest of grand balls, paid for by the grateful British government, and attended by King Louis XVIII and all the Allies. Lady Frances, in an advanced state of pregnancy, took her seat on the top table at Wellington's right hand. The great man theatrically delayed his entrance until the last moment, milking prodigious applause.

On the Duke's left sat Lady Caroline Lamb, already hard at work in daylight hours on *Glenarvon*, a Gothic novel that would be published the following year. It included scathing caricatures of the patronesses, one of whom, Lady Jersey, cancelled Lady Caroline's vouchers to Almack's in retaliation. Although Amelia loathed her sister-in-law, when Caroline was barred from Almack's, a deep social disgrace that reflected on the whole family, she moved heaven and earth over the next two years to have the ban lifted.

The Duchess of Richmond, marooned in Brussels, where the stink of unburied corpses at Waterloo wafted through the summer air, could only seethe in absentia at the frantic socialising in the French capital. She was in 'a grand fuss to get to Paris' but Richmond, even more impecunious than usual, was 'very much adverse' to the idea. When he finally gave in, the Richmonds travelled by coach from Brussels with four of their daughters, the duchess hoping the autumn season would bear fruit in the marriage market. But in a twist worthy of *Pride and Prejudice*, it turned out that the 23-year-old Lady Sarah Lennox had been conducting a clandestine affair with Maitland. This 38-year-old widower was increasingly attractive to a much younger woman as the officer commanding the 1st Brigade of Guards, who had hurled back Napoleon's Imperial Guard in the death-or-glory finale to Waterloo. The pair had been seen dancing together a little too frequently at the ball but at the time the duchess's mind had been elsewhere.

For Maitland, who had neither wealth nor title but was now in charge of the Paris garrison, the arrival of the Richmonds *en famille* offered an irresistible opportunity. He took his beloved under cover of darkness to the home of the Reverend Stonestreet, who had marched all the way to Paris with the guards. Maitland thought he could reply on his chaplain's unquestioning support. Much to the major-general's consternation, however, it was not forthcoming. At 7.30 p.m. on 15 October, a sobbing Lady Sarah, sitting in the back of a fiacre, a Parisian hackney cab, heard the Reverend lecture Maitland on the doorstep about 'mad capers of intrigues'. Stonestreet, alluding to the amicable blacksmith of Gretna Green, the spiritual home of elopements, declared he 'would not become the blacksmith' of Paris. Off went the couple in a vain search for a more compliant chaplain. The following morning, Lady Sarah now hopelessly compromised, having slept in Maitland's rooms overnight, Wellington himself intervened.

'With a piece of Generalship not very honourable', as the good reverend indignantly put it, the Duke tricked Stonestreet into preparing the marriage licence, backdated to 9 October, when Lady Sarah had entered Paris, and ordered his own chaplain to conduct the ceremony. Richmond had to break the bad news to his furious wife. Her friend and rival Caroline Capel, before long gleefully circulating details of the scandal to the Brussels set, said 'The Duchess's high hopes are dashed to the Ground, and will not I fear improve her *gentle* temper'. Her husband confided in Stonestreet that 'he had been long enough in Paris and wish'd himself back, and at Brussels'.

Lady Caroline Capel gleefully circulated news of the Duchess of Richmond's discomfiture. There was little love lost between them, especially as the Capels, although also economic exiles, could afford to rent a much more palatial residence in the centre of Brussels

(opposite) Major-General Sir Peregrine Maitland, commander of the First Foot Guards, who repelled the final French attacks at Waterloo. In September 1815 Maitland took advantage of the arrival of the Richmond family in Paris, where he was garrison commander, to elope with the Duchess of Richmond's daughter, Lady Sarah Lennox

Maitland was appointed Lieutenant-Governor of Upper Canada, and settled down with Lady Sarah in an idyllic 22-room summer house built for them a few kilometres from Niagara Falls. They would have ten children: three boys, seven girls. Richmond repaid Wellington for his kindly intervention by perjuring himself at a libel trial. Permitted as a peer of the realm a reassuringly comfortable seat next to the judge, he denied newspaper allegations and described Wellington's mistress, Lady Frances, as a lady of unimpeachable virtue. The jury's less than generous award of damages suggested room for considerable doubt.

In 1819, with paid employment at last as the new Governor-General of Canada, the duke toured the country with his two eldest daughters. Richmond visited the Maitlands near Niagara and took pride in showing them the map he had kept in his possession since the night of the ball, with the indent clearly made by Wellington's thumbnail just below the village of Waterloo. At Fort William Henry in Quebec Province Richmond, coming to the aid of his pet spaniel, Blücher, was bitten on the hand by a fox. He dismissed the injury as trivial at the time but hydrophobia developed rapidly and on 28 August the duke died in extreme agony from rabies in a barn a few miles from a settlement that had been named in his honour. In all the horror and confusion, the famous map he had preserved so carefully was never seen again.

If Richmond's was the grimmest death, that of Castlereagh was the strangest. In May 1822 he threatened to resign as Foreign Secretary when his wife Emily, constantly at loggerheads with George IV's last mistress, Elizabeth Marchionesse of Conyngham, found she had been left off the guest list of an official dinner and dance to be held in honour of the Crown Prince of Denmark. Countess Lieven, as often was the case, unintentionally or otherwise, fanned the flames of discontent. She tried to bring both ladies together but reported that Emily 'gave me the slip'. 'I am furious', she told Castlereagh, whose own problems were mounting. On 9 August the Foreign Secretary was granted an audience with the king and claimed the police had a warrant out for his arrest on charges of homosexuality. He showed the king two blackmailers' letters, one of which threatened to expose his 'irregular conduct' to his wife and the other 'concerning a more terrible subject'. Back in 1819, Castlereagh had been enticed to a transvestite brothel and his identity exposed and had 'emptied his wallet' to keep it a secret. Two years later virtually the same thing happened to his private secretary, Richard Meade, 3rd Earl of Clanwilliam; and therein may lie the key. Meade had been brought up in Vienna, spoke German and French fluently, and at the age of 19 as a young diplomat had accompanied Castlereagh to the Congress. His friendship with Castlereagh was intimate, perhaps sexually intimate, and the Foreign Secretary's marriage was childless. As to the 'more terrible subject', on 16 January 1788 Castlereagh admitted to his step-grandfather, Lord Camden, that he had caught a sexually transmitted disease while a student at Cambridge University and had therefore moved to 'solitary lodgings', which, in an all-male environment, was implicit of an effort on his part to contain and cease homosexual promiscuity. As the disease progressed, it would have affected eye and muscle coordination, which might explain why an expert marksman such as Castlereagh had all but missed Canning in their 1806 duel. Seeing conspiracies everywhere and telling both the king and Wellington that he had 'gone mad', on 11 August 1822 Castlereagh committed suicide, cutting the carotid artery in his neck with a penknife.

Byron, who despite his brilliance seems to have been a thoroughly nasty piece of work, penned a vitriolic epitaph to Castlereagh:

'So he has cut his throat at last. He? Who?
The man who cut his country's long ago.'

Castlereagh committed suicide in 1822 by cutting his own throat. The event was recorded by George Cruikshank but the sketch lacked his usual zest

Clanwilliam refused to serve with Castlereagh's successor as Foreign Secretary, his inveterate enemy, George Canning. Castlereagh and Canning had remained at loggerheads until the last. Canning was thought to be behind Queen Caroline's decision to reside in the house next door to Castlereagh in St James' Square in 1820 when the government tried and failed to persuade parliament to pass a bill that would allow George IV to divorce his queen. Castlereagh for his part raked up an old (and probably true) scandal that Canning had been the queen's lover, according to Castlereagh, 'one of the many favoured'. The following year the queen was barred from Westminster Abbey for the coronation and died shortly afterwards. Castlereagh received a state funeral despite his suicide. Leading members of the Cabinet, with Canning conspicuous by his absence, carried the coffin into Westminster Abbey. In 1827 Canning would achieve his ambition and become Prime Minister but his health was failing. He died in office after 119 days, the shortest term on record.

Wellington, the father of the nation, was still attending balls, garden parties and banquets in his honour at the age of 80. Only once did the conqueror of Bonaparte suffer a serious setback. William Mackall left Almack's to his niece, whose husband, John Willis, took on the job of manager and on ball nights, doorkeeper. Early in 1821, the Duke drove up in his carriage, five minutes after eleven o'clock, the latest permissible entry time, to find the front door firmly shut. He gave a thunderous knock: Willis opened it the merest crack and was sent off to find Lady Jersey. 'What time is it, Willis?' said she, knowing the answer. 'Seven minutes past, milady', said Willis. 'Keep him out!' was her answer. Willis did not relish returning to give such a message to the hero of Waterloo. He tried again: 'He has been debating in the House of Lords, milady.' Her reply was swift and final: 'Let the Lords meet earlier on an Almack's night'. The scene was played out in front of an incredulous gentleman named Herbert Tricknor, who dined out for weeks on the story afterwards. Upon hearing the verdict, nervously delivered by Willis, the Duke drew his military cloak about his person and stepped back into his carriage. Almost as an afterthought, he lowered the window and said, 'So much for the discipline of petticoat government!'

The English writer Pierce Eagan, putting the finishing touches to the first edition of his *Life in London*, had just time to add this humorous postscript:

> *'My Lord, you have enough to do,*
> *ALMACK'S is not like WATERLOO.'*

Charlotte, Duchess of Richmond, did not travel to North America with her husband. She had her hands full with her youngest daughter, Lady Georgiana, who remained in Paris when the rest of the family returned to Brussels. She was said to be seriously ill but her sisters spitefully suggested another explanation. Her dalliance with the Duke may have resulted in a pregnancy, perhaps a miscarriage. Georgy was always Wellington's favourite. After she had been packed off to stay with an aunt, Lady Georgiana Bathurst, Wellington corresponded regularly from Paris. On 1 February 1817 he wrote: 'I gave a brilliant ball on the 29th [January]. It only wanted you to be perfect.'

Georgy may have hoped that Wellington would divorce his wife. She did not marry until 1924, at the age of 29. It was an unpromising match with her cousin, William Lennox Lascelles Fitzgerald de Ros. He inaugurated rowing at Christ Church College, Oxford, where Ros remained for a record nine years as an undergraduate, frequently admonished for his indolence and absence. William was a third son but somewhat against the odds, would succeed to the family title as 23rd Baron de Ros of Helmsley. This did not prevent him from becoming the most notorious officer in the British Army. On the eve of the Crimean War he was appointed quartermaster general and sent to Varna on the Black Sea coast to prepare for the arrival of the British expeditionary force. A devoted enthusiast for sun bathing, he got sunstroke and was invalided back to Britain, the first recorded such casualty. Poor Georgy had a hapless incompetent to care for, when she had wanted a hero. Georgy was always in the bloom of health herself and lived to the age of 96.

Her mother took the dreadful news of the Duke of Richmond's awful death calmly and never married again. Her hand-to-mouth existence ended dramatically in 1836, when she inherited the huge Gordon estates upon the death of her brother, George Gordon, 5th Duke of Gordon, who had left no legitimate children. Charlotte, cantankerous to the last, remembered with affection in her will only her housekeeper, Ann Meade, and her butler, Frederick Collett. She died in London on 5 May 1842, aged 73.

Chapter Ten

The Last Waltz

BONAPARTE was indeed sent to St. Helena, where he died on 5 May, 1821. In his will he left Lady Holland a gold snuff box given to him in 1797 by Pope Pius VI for sparing Rome and 150,000 francs to Georgine de la Chastellux and her son. There would be no second Hundred Days. Napoleon's final defeat at Waterloo allowed the Austrians, who had only one significant victory over the French, at Aspern-Essling in May 1809, to concentrate on what they did best. The favoured sons of Austria were not generals such as Wellington but composers like Mozart, Beethoven and Strauss.

This enamelled and cameo-set snuff box was left to Lady Holland by Napoleon in his will. He wrote a note to accompany his bequest on the back of a playing card, expressing his gratitude for her help in 1814-15

Heinrich Laube, German dramatist and highly successful theatre director in Vienna.
Alluding to Austria's preference for music over munitions, he described Strauss the Elder
as their heroic equivalent to Napoleon

Nearly half a century later the German dramatist, novelist and theatre director, Heinriche Laube, still thought it fashionable to mock the Austrians gently. Invited to a splendid Viennese ball, he gestured towards the orchestra and a certain celebrated conductor, and said:

'There stands the modern hero of Austria, Le Napoleon Austrichien, Johann Strauss. The Strauss waltzes are to the Viennese what Napoleon's victories were to the French.'

Two men entirely without lineage or pretensions now shared the title of Father of the Viennese Waltz: Joseph Lanner and Johann Strauss the Elder. Lanner was born in April 1801, the son of a glove maker. By the age of 12, he was playing violin with a popular dance band and at 17 formed his own trio of two violins and a guitar. Johann Strauss I, born in March 1804, had the tougher upbringing. He was the son of an innkeeper who committed suicide when Strauss was just 12, by throwing himself into the River Danube. The two men got together in 1823 when Lanner, hearing Strauss play the viola, added him to his group.

Johann Strauss I (left) and Joseph Lanner, who shared the title of Father of the Viennese Waltz, both came from humble origins. Lanner was the son of a glove maker and Strauss of an innkeeper who committed suicide by throwing himself in the Danube when his son was aged 12

They were soon inseparable, sharing the proceeds of gigs, debts, houses, girls and even their shirts. On one occasion, down to their last clean shirt, they took turns wearing it. Lanner wore it first, while Strauss stayed home. In September 1825 the 'melting, sentimental' Lanner and the 'fiery, stormy' Strauss had a very public falling out. The press said that Lanner had introduced some waltzes as though they were his when in fact they had been composed by Strauss. The real reason was much more mundane: Strauss had stolen a girl that Lanner, for once, actually cared about. At the end of a concert at the *Zum Bok* [The Ram] ballroom, Lanner gave an over-indulgent speech of thanks, which Strauss brought to an abrupt ending by hitting him with his violin bow. Both men were the worse for drink and tired and Lanner lashed back at Strauss. As things got completely out of hand, they began to smash their instruments on each other, followed by pieces of furniture. One chair, allegedly thrown by Strauss, although he denied it afterwards, missed Lanner and shattered the magnificent mirror behind him, pride and joy of the *Zum Bok* and famous throughout Vienna, sending splinters of glass over the audience. This sobered both men up and they quickly left the building.

In 1848 Johann Strauss I played in England, where he was one of a series of famous visitors to an even more famous exile, Metternich. Marginalised in domestic politics, the great statesman's vanity was his undoing. He took responsibility for decrees that he did not sign or support and became a hated symbol of repression. When the tides of reaction swept around Europe, Metternich had to resign - on 13 March, the first victim of the revolution.

After a traumatic flight via Germany and Holland, he took a house at number 44 Eaton Square in London and was seen queuing at Almack's for a ballroom ticket for his third wife, Countess Melanie Zichy-Ferraris. The Duke of Wellington, nearly eighty, kept him entertained but Metternich had almost no money. The Austrian government accused him of fiddling his expenses and stopped his pension. He was forced to move to Brighton, pursued by a string of geriatric (although Wellington put it in much ruder terms) former mistresses, including Dorothea Lieven and Princess Bagration. After eighteen months the new political force in Vienna, Prince Felix of Schwarzenberg, allowed Metternich to return and go into less than graceful retirement.

Strauss took sixteen of Lanner's musicians with him and formed his own orchestra. The pair were reconciled in 1828 when Strauss made an unscheduled appearance at the wedding reception of Lanner's daughter, which by chance took place in the *Zum Bok* ballroom. The two men embraced one another 'amid shouts and tears of joy'. Thereafter they met frequently and played each other's compositions. Two orchestras were even more successful than one. In September 1831 Frédérick Chopin arrived in Vienna hoping to exploit his own composing skills. Within days he realised 'Lanner, Strauss and their waltzes dominate everything' and left for Paris.

In 1843, Lanner succumbed on Good Friday to a typhus epidemic raging through Vienna. Strauss conducted the music at his funeral.

Much less easily resolved was the relationship between Strauss and his sons. He did not want them to become musicians and once thrashed Johann Strauss Junior for secretly learning to play the violin. Born one month after his father broke away from Lanner's orchestra, Johann Strauss II continued to study, with the help of his mother, Anna. By age 19 he had become Strauss Senior's chief competitor, or would have, if the ballroom proprietors had been prepared to risk offending his powerful father. On October 15, 1844, *Dommayer's* casino, bankrolled by Anna, took the risk of hosting the new younger Strauss orchestra. Tickets were at an absolute premium and in the crush, many women were hurt or simply fainted. At first Strauss II was overcome with stage fright but recovered and soon won over his audience. A Strauss I supporter reported back to the glowering patriarch, 'Your son was terrific.' They did not speak for two years. Then, on the night of 23 June, 1846, Johann Junior gathered with a small group of musicians under the window of his father's bedroom and began to serenade him with his own waltzes. The old man cracked. After Strauss I died in 1851, Johann II conducted his father's orchestra in a memorial concert.

With his brothers Josef and Eduard, Johann II became the first to exploit the financial potential of Viennese balls. They encouraged 'Strauss benefits', a form of commercial sponsorship, organised collections – for themselves - and insisted on admission fees. Josef was the brains of Team Strauss, but also an accomplished conductor in his own right. In 1870 he went to Warsaw to conduct a Viennese orchestra, whose instruments were left on a train, forcing Josef to find local musicians as replacements. The first violinist lost his way, musical chaos ensued, and Josef collapsed on the stage, fell down a flight of steps and suffered a severe concussion. Johann rushed to Warsaw to find his brother in a coma and although he recovered consciousness for a brief time, Josef died in Vienna soon afterwards, at the age of 43. Their brother Eduard, also a talented conductor and composer, took over the administrative side of the business.

The casino created by Ferdinand Dommayer, where Strauss the Younger first branched out on his own, to the fury of his father

Strauss the Younger left nothing to chance, preparing for his performances as meticulously as a modern television producer and ensuring that his face appeared on huge number of promotional posters. His precise play list for a royal ball from the 1860s survives, with the timings of every dance noted down to the last second.

Strauss II had a glittering career, with international fame on the scale of the Beatles whenever he went on tour. In 1872, after sailing to New York, he was the star of the Boston Music Festival, whose great coliseum was specially built for the occasion. Inside, Strauss conducted 900 of the finest musicians, brought together from across America. There was rapturous applause for his most famous waltz, *On The Beautiful Blue Danube*, which curiously had been a flop in 1867 on its first performance in Vienna. Strauss said at that time: 'The devil take my waltz... I wish it had been a success!" He need not have worried. The work sold millions and his signature on the surviving musical score from the opening bars of the *Blue Danube* is one of the world's most valuable examples of sheet music.

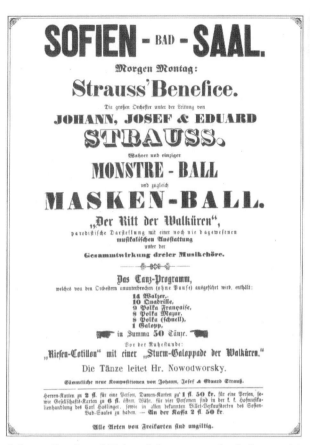

A 'benefit' for Johann, Josef and Eduard Strauss at the Sofien-saal in 1863.
It promised the participants 14 waltzes

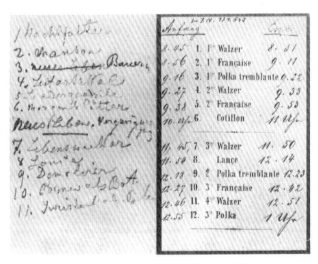

The play list for a royal ball, showing that Johann Strauss II timed meticulously
every performance

Johann Strauss II depicted in the Viennese satirical magazine, 'Der Floh ('the Flea') in 1869. 'Der Floh' appeared on Sundays from 1869 to 1919

In 1872 Strauss II was the star of the Boston Music Festival, whose great coliseum was built specially for the event. Strauss conducted 900 talented musicians assembled from across America

A rare card signed by Strauss on which he also added an excerpt from the musical score of the Blue Danube Waltz

Johann Strauss's most famous waltz,' On The Beautiful Blue Danube', inexplicably was a flop when first performed in Vienna in 1867

The demand for balls in Vienna far exceeded the available space in the Hofburg and other ballrooms were built in the city. By far the largest was the Apollo-saal. Inside, it was like something out of ancient Rome, full of exotic statues, triumphal arches and marble pillars. The Apollo-saal had five enormous ballrooms, forty-four large drawing-rooms, three vast conservatories and thirteen kitchens. Even in the depths of winter, marvellous greenery and flowers adorned the paths that led to waterfalls and grottoes, and a lake with real swans on it.

(above & overleaf) The Apollo-saal, Vienna's largest venue, which looked like something out of ancient Rome. The Apollo-saal had five ballrooms and a lake with real swans on it

One chandelier in the biggest ballroom held 5,000 candles, which may account for the Apollo-saal catching alight and burning down in 1876, despite the best efforts of the conspicuously ill-equipped and unresponsive Viennese Fire Brigade. This left the Sofien Saal, favourite venue of Johann Strauss II, as the pre-eminent ballroom. This survived long into the twentieth century before it went into decline and eventually became a disco. In August 2001 the Sofien Saal also

Der grose Apollo Saal mit Ansicht des Eintrittsaales.

caught fire and only its facade survived. At one point the fire brigade ran out of water, which was rather ironic as the building had started life as a swimming pool.

The waltz had become so fashionable in nineteenth century Vienna that the leading restaurants were compelled to set aside areas for dance floors to keep their clientele. Each dance floor, however small, needed an ensemble. There was such a shortage of violinists in Vienna, they were recruited from as far away as the Tyrol.

Some musicians became celebrated in their own right, including the hugely talented Schrammel brothers. Johann aged 9, and Joseph aged 11, became solo violinists and raised the funds they needed to enrol at the renowned Vienna Conservatory for music lessons by playing in the street. In 1884, at the height of their fame, they formed a quartet, which created what became known throughout Europe as 'Schrammel music'. Their compositions, especially for the waltz, would have received far more recognition had they been arranged for a full orchestra. But the Schrammel brothers were hopeless with money and fell on hard times. Both died comparatively young, at the age of 42.

The Schrammel quartet, so good that Johann Strauss went to hear them play.
The Schrammel brothers fell on hard times and died young

The younger Strauss often went to hear the Schrammels perform for his own amusement and Crown Prince Rudolph of Austria became their patron until the great mystery of Mayerling. In January 1889 Josef Bratfisch, the royal coachman of Crown Prince Rudolf, brought the Prince's mistress, Baroness Mary Vetsera, to Mayerling, the royal hunting lodge 24 kilometres south-west of Vienna. Baroness Vetsera was the 17-year old daughter of a diplomat at the Viennese court. A day later, they were dead. After their bodies were discovered, it was announced that the lovers had decided on a suicide pact. The Prince allegedly first shot the Baroness and sat by her body for several hours before shooting himself. No one is sure what really happened but Bratfisch was said to have received an income for life for keeping quiet about what he knew and shortly afterwards he retired to breed horses. In the sanitised version, a rival for the Baroness's affections, Georg Baltazzi, arrived at Mayerling and allegedly killed the Crown Prince in the cellar by a blow to the temple with a champagne bottle. He was forced to leave Austria, and went to the United States. The Baroness did not die but allegedly was sent into exile in Bohemia. The Austrian Emperor was heard to say that any version was better than the real thing.

On less violent occasions, passengers were content to ask a Viennese coachman for a 'porcelain ride', which meant calm and steady. This was almost obligatory in the nineteenth century when between balls carriages were often used to move precious porcelain from one place to another. From 1860 to 1900 the carriage trade boomed in Vienna, with more than 1,000 fiakers, named after the French for hackney carriage, all numbered, roaming the city streets. The coachmen were noted for their discretion, especially when transporting a gentleman with his paramour – often in a closed carriage that simply went round in circles with the blinds down.

Mayerling hunting lodge, scene of the mysterious suicide of the Schrammels'
patron, Crown Prince Rudolph

The real scandal in Vienna was the depth of anti-Semitism, condoned and encouraged by many foreign residents, and the level of sexual exploitation of young dancers. One former British army officer, who regularly took leave in Austria in the early 1870s, said of those employed at the Hofopern, Vienna's state opera house, 'even the quite young ones from twelve to thirteen years old have intrigues; all this is an open secret, which the ladies in high society speak about'. In an anonymous book of *Society Recollections* the officer was irrevocably condemned out of his own mouth. 'I knew a young fair girl of thirteen who really was quite a remarkable beauty', he wrote, 'their code of morality is quite different from ours … if an Austrian lady were fast they thought nothing of it, as they were all fast… They think it the most natural thing in the world for a girl to have lovers'. Hebephilia, the sexual preference for children in early puberty, was combined with outrageous anti-Semitic assumptions and prejudices. In this officer's view, 'Austrian women, and more particularly the Viennese, age very soon… I have noticed this particularly with the Jewesses, who at twelve or thirteen years are as developed as English girls of fifteen or sixteen; but they fade as rapidly, besides becoming excessively stout'.

The Hofopern-Theater took eight years to complete and opened in May 1869. However, the opera impresarios wanted nothing to do with vulgar waltzes. The Emperor himself had to intervene before the Hofopern would agree to host a state ball, the Opernball, in December 1877.

The state opera house dancers in 1906. Many of the younger girls were sexually exploited

Russian tanks roll through Vienna in 1945. The state opera house was almost destroyed by bombing

Only in 1935 did the Opernball become official –for just four years, until the outbreak of the Second World War. The Opera House was almost destroyed by bombing in 1945 and soon afterwards Russian troops arrived in Vienna. The Vienna Opera Ball had to wait for the Opera House to be rebuilt and the ball was not held again until 1956.

Since then, with one exception, it has become an annual event, described by one Austrian newspaper as the most famous, most legendary, most decadent ball in the world, attended by 5,000 guests. Held in February each year, the ball takes over the state Opera House for a single, Thursday night. To minimise the time for which the opera has to be closed and there are no performances, hundreds of workers labour for 36 hours to remove all the seating and obstacles at ground level. They then lay a parquet floor, linking what is usually the auditorium with the stage, to create a single, spectacular, level, continuous surface. You could fit 25 coach maker's barns of the size that held the Duchess of Richmond's Ball into the same space.

A vast stage is prepared for Vienna's annual Opera Ball held in February

Friction, in the literal sense, is a key consideration in performing the Viennese waltz at the Opera Ball. Constant pivoting from one toe and heel to the other requires proper friction between dancing shoes and dance floor. The Viennese waltz evolved a time when most shoes were made of leather and the dance floors were bare boards, slightly worn, providing the ideal friction for dancing. The Opera House Ball's floor is almost smooth, making the waltz that much more demanding. As a consequence, centrifugal force plays a pivotal part in their Viennese waltz. The only way for dancers not to grow tired very quickly is to ensure that their arms and feet are properly positioned, as they whirl against the centrifugal force produced by their movements.

The Ball's unique feature is the young ladies of Austrian society, the debutantes. In the United Kingdom debutantes ceased to be presented to the Queen after 1957, a near fatal blow to their existence; but in Austria the debutantes continue to thrive because of the State Opera Ball.

Almost all of them are trained in the art of dance and etiquette at Vienna's famous Elmayer Dance School. It was founded in 1917 by Willi Elmayer, a former captain in the dragoons, and produced its first graduates in 1919. From the very beginning the school was located in the old Pallavicini Palace stables, next to the stables of the Spanish Riding School – the home of the famous white stallions in the centre of Vienna.

For this occasion of a lifetime, Elmayer's best pupils are put through their paces like stallions. Even with a degree in dancing, to be a debutante at the Vienna Opera Ball, candidates must formally register to have any chance at all of being accepted. The Viennese waltz is given absolute priority at auditions for the ball and the candidates are required to follow strict guidelines. Only those who are capable of proficiently dancing the Viennese waltz counter-clockwise will pass the audition.

This is because the opening dance at the Opera Ball, with an extraordinary 186 couples dancing the Viennese waltz together, is the supreme moment of truth. The experts say that no other dance is as magical, harder to perfect or as fulfilling.

When a couple dances it correctly, they experience an aerial gliding effect, helping them to manoeuvre across the dance floor as though no-one else is there. A true Viennese waltz has a natural turn that rotates to the right, followed by reverse turns, rotates to the left, and change steps to redirect the rotation. Couples dance continuously in a counter-clockwise movement around the dance floor, each couple following the other at almost warp speed and yet never making the mistake of passing each other.

In the old Opera House the Opera Ball had much less room for its opening waltz.
This picture was taken in February 1939, the last ball before the Second World War

The debutantes' waltz at the Opera Ball, a blurred memory of perpetual motion, is their
supreme moment of truth. No other dance is as magical, harder to perfect or as fulfilling

Probably the Opera Ball's most successful chair, Elizabeth Gürtler, for six years combined the role with that of chief executive of the Hotel Sacher, which she assumed in 1990 following the suicide of her ex-husband, Peter Gürtler. Some saw her arrival as a parallel with events in the Sacher's chequered past. In 1882 the Sacher had been a failing establishment when Anna Sacher, the wife of owner Franz Sacher, took over as general manager, at the age of 23. Despite her youth, she overcame great hostility and cynicism in what was then a man's world, and transformed the Sacher into the most luxurious and successful hotel in Vienna. She was fond of big cigars and small dogs, and kept both in large numbers in her apartment in the hotel. Unfortunately after World War I Anna's refusal to allow the hotel to cater for guests who lacked what she considered to be the requisite pedigree, while unwisely granting extended credit to impoverished aristocrats, led to the bankruptcy of the Sacher and its sale to the Gürtlers in 1934. Anna's husband Franz had first opened the hotel sixty years previously but was only interested in his cakes. In 1832, at the age of 16, as a young pastry chef, he created the legendary sacher torte for a dinner party hosted by Metternich. The exact recipe of his exquisite chocolate cake, with its thin layer of apricot jam, remains a carefully guarded secret.

Anna Sacher (overleaf), one of the first women to succeed in the male dominated nineteenth century world of hotel management. Her hotel (above) the Sacher, was the most luxurious in Vienna

Frau **Adele Strauss** gibt im eigenen, sowie im Namen der Geschwister **Eduard Strauss**, k. k. Hofballmusik-Director, **Anna Strauss** und **Therese Strauss** gebrochenen Herzens Nachricht von dem Hinscheiden ihres innigstgeliebten Mannes, resp. Bruders, des Herrn

Johann Strauss,

des besten, edelsten Menschen, des zärtlichsten Gatten und hingebungsvollsten Freundes.

Mit den Tröstungen der Religion versehen, ist er S a m s t a g d e n 3. J u n i nach kurzem schweren Leiden im 74. Lebensjahre sanft in dem Herrn entschlafen.

Das Leichenbegängniss findet D i e n s t a g d e n 6. J u n i um 3 Uhr N a c h m i t t a g s vom Trauerhause : IV., I g e l g a s s e N r. 4, aus statt.

Die Einsegnung erfolgt um ¹/₂4 Uhr in der evangelischen Kirche A. B., I., Dorotheergasse 18.

Die Leiche wird sodann auf den Centralfriedhof überführt und dortselbst beigesetzt.

WIEN, am 4. Juni 1899.   11165

The death notice for Johann Strauss II. At his funeral, his violin rested on a red velvet cushion behind the casket

As the nineteenth century gave way to the twentieth, the waltz said goodbye to its most brilliant star. On 3 June 1899 Johann Strauss II was working on a score for *Cinderella* when he fell into a sleep from which he would never wake. An hour later the news of his death reached Eduard Kremser, who was conducting a benefit concert in the Stadtpark pavilion to raise money for a monument to honour Joseph Lanner and Strauss the Elder. He stopped the orchestra and began instead to conduct *On The Beautiful Blue Danube*. The audience, at first perplexed, realised its significance and unashamedly wept. Three days later they lined the streets of Vienna in silence as Johann II's coffin was carried in a funeral procession, with the maestro's violin resting on a red velvet pillow immediately behind the casket.

In 1936 Josef Goebbels is said to have contributed to the funds of the embryonic Strauss Society, formed to collect and preserve the music of Johann Strauss II. Two years later, however, it emerged that Strauss's Aryan bloodline, heralded by the Nazis, was far from pure. Strauss's great-great-grandfather was Jewish and so was his wife, Adele.

After Austria was absorbed into the Third Reich, music scholars who knew the truth were threatened with deportation to concentration camps if they broke their silence; marriage documents containing information about his Jewish heritage were destroyed and forgeries with a fictitious family tree created to replace them. The music of Johann II had been widely used in German propaganda films to symbolise the purity of their race.

This left only one undiscovered secret: the composer of *On The Beautiful Blue Danube*, Johann Strauss, could not waltz.

Chapter Eleven

A Twist in the Tale

IN THE FEBRILE ATMOSPHERE of post-Waterloo Paris, General Maitland's occupying force of long-suffering British regulars is saving the city from the Prussians and the Prussians from its citizens. Marshal Blucher, who suffered a blow to the head before Waterloo, is growing increasingly irrational. He orders the Pont Jena to be blown to smithereens. It has a single British sentry whose life is preserved only by the incompetence of the sappers whose charges fail to explode. With Maitland somewhat distracted by his new young bride, mistakes begin to happen. Two Prussian officers ignore Maitland's warnings and visit the brothels. They fail to report for duty the next day. Weeks later, their decomposing bodies are found at the bottom of a well. Rumbling ominously just beneath the surface is the Parisian underworld that took up 'La Marseillaise ', the Strasbourg song adopted by the volunteers marching from Marseille to save the Revolution. 'Aux armes, citoyens!'

All the major chess pieces in the Great Game remained in play in the summer of 1815. Ambassador Wellington had determined on a political career: realistically there was no one left that Britain was capable of defeating on the battlefield. The Americans had already given their old colonial masters a bloody nose and the Russians, as Napoleon discovered to his cost, always had Generals January and February on their side. The Czar himself remained a loose cannon with no patience for diplomacy. Metternich was still pulling the strings in central Europe. Talleyrand clung to power in France despite the double changing of the guard.

And behind most of them lurked the shadowy figure of Joseph Fouché, who would go to any lengths to make himself useful to the winning side without completely severing his ties with the losers. Fouché's instincts, though, were those of ruthless fanaticism. In Year Two of the Revolution, he had mowed down more than 1,500 citizens of Lyon with a cannon packed with grapeshot. Fouché voted for the execution of Louis XVI. He was the former president of the notorious Jacobin Club. More often and not, whatever the colour of the French government, Fouché somehow managed to remain in charge of a police force more akin to the Gestapo than the Bow Street Runners. After Napoleon's first abdication he made himself indispensable to Talleyrand, who persuaded Luis XVIII to appoint to him minister of police, the very man who had decreed the decapitation of his own brother. During the Hundred Days Fouché sold military secrets to both sides, using his vast spy network established under the Empire. When the Bourbons returned in July 1815, in order to ingratiate himself with the ultra-loyalists Fouché compiled lists of proscribed people to be kept out of office, imprisoned, or in a few instances, charged with treason. It was an echo of the real Terror during the Revolution and swept a big fish, Charles de la Bédoyère, into his net.

(opposite) The Traitors' Club: a caricature of the Revolution shows Fouché and Lavalette among the interrogators of luckless members of the aristocracy after the massacre at Lyon

After his arrest Charles was interrogated at the prefecture de police for two days, led by the baby-faced Etienne Decazes, who reported directly to Fouché. Some of the sessions continued into the small hours. Then without warning la Bédoyère was transferred under cover of darkness to the much more secure military prison known as l'Abbaye. The Chastellux family, correctly fearing appeals to the authorities would fall on deaf ears, set about planning his escape. They established that Marcel Warmé, the concierge at l'Abbaye, was prepared to provide duplicate keys for a vast down payment of 20,000 francs and four further payments of 20,000 francs. What Warmé insisted on however was a cover story that made the escape look as if it resulted from the negligence of the garrison. As ideas gradually took shape, they decided that Georgine would make one of her regular routine visits and instead of leaving the prison, would be hidden in a storeroom by Warmé for a few hours. At the critical moment, she would return to la Bédoyère's cell and remain there while he made his way out of l'Abbaye during the night using the duplicate keys. Upon her discovery in the morning, Georgine would claim that Charles, dressed in women's clothes she had brought him, had left the prison undetected, quite openly, in her place.

However the stratagem was never put into effect. La Bédoyère refused to countenance any proposal that he believed would damage his military reputation. He may also have feared for his wife's safety when she was discovered. And unbeknown to Georgine, Charles had received a letter from the old lady most influential in his life. Miss Plunkett urged him on no account to agree to try to escape. If needs be, she believed he had to die for the cause of Bonapartism and liberty: *I'll faut qu'il périsse.*

On the same day, 19 August 1815, that la Bédoyère faced the firing squad, Marshal Michel Ney was brought back to Paris to face charges of treason. Having seen Charles's fate in front of a military tribunal, Ney opted instead to be tried by The House of Peers (to which both he and la Bédoyère belonged). It must have been an unpleasant shock when the royalist peers found him guilty on 7 December and put him in front of a firing squad only a few hours later.

In the meantime comte Pierre de Lavalette, Minister for Posts under Napoleon, was also sentenced to death on 21 November. The night before his scheduled execution, he was visited at the Conciergerie prison near the Île de la Cité by a family group including his 13-year-old daughter and his spouse, Emilie de Beauharnais, niece of Napoleon's first wife, Josephine. Emilie used the ruse abandoned by Georgine. Lavalette changed clothes and places with his wife.

*(pages 166, 167 & 168) Georgine de Chastellux pleads in vain with the King of France
for her husband's life;
Marshal Ney bears his breast before his firing squad;
Lavalette's family spirit him out of jail disguised as a woman. The artist made the
connection between the three events and the pictures endured, even appearing in French
school text books as late as 1906*

She was a brave woman. Only weeks earlier she had lost the baby she was carrying. The Parisian press carried an excited account of the moment of discovery:

In the meantime Madame de Lavalette, who had thrown over her the large cloak belonging to her husband to escape earlier detection, was seated, breathless, in his armchair in his cell, with a book in her hand, and the candle burning behind her on a table. At half past 6 in the morning a gaoler, entering the room, spoke to her, but met with no reply; he repeated the question, and, astonished at the continued silence, he approached nearer to the Lady, when, with a smile, succeeded by strong convulsions, she exclaimed 'Il est parti!'

Emilie was badly beaten up by Lavalette's warders. She was then arrested and despite a clamour for her release, she remained in prison until 23 January 1816.

Lavalette escaped to England by way of Mons, aided and abetted by two British officers, Robert Thomas Wilson, a lieutenant-colonel, and John Hely-Hutchinson, a captain in Maitland's 1st foot guards and a future Irish peer. The key player in its execution, however, was a 32-year-old British businessman, Michael Bruce. For three weeks he hid Lavalette in his smart Paris apartment, while the French police all but tore down the slums in an unsuccessful search for him. All three conspirators were arrested, charged with helping a convicted prisoner to escape. Despite the seriousness of the crime, they were sentenced to a derisory ninety days' imprisonment following British diplomatic pressure.

The escape committee who sprung Lavalette: (left to right) Bruce, Wilson and Hely-Hutchinson

Bruce, known thereafter as 'Lavalette Bruce', had been conducting a secret affair with Ney's wife Louise, or as Wilson wryly put it, imminent widow. If Wilson were not the inspiration for Major Michael Hogan, the snuff-taking eminence grise in the Richard Sharpe novels, then he certainly ought to have been. The grandson of a Leeds cloth merchant, and orphaned at the age of twelve, Wilson was a brilliant tactician and bold cavalry officer. After Alexander and Napoleon made peace in 1807, the Russians expelled Wilson as a spy, which undoubtedly he was. But by 1812 Britain and Russia were on the same side. Wilson, newly accredited as a liaison officer with the Russians, became one of only a handful of foreign eye witnesses to the disastrous French retreat. He spent most of the intervening years as an aide to Wellington in the Peninsula War, one of the few officers the Duke allowed to improvise. During the Waterloo campaign, he gathered vital intelligence on Napoleon's intentions. It is almost inconceivable that Wilson's participation in the escape of Lavalette in 1815 took place without Wellington's knowledge and approval.

In January 1819 a French officer sailed from Bordeaux to Charleston on a cargo ship. A veteran of Waterloo, also on board, thought he recognised the man but could not be certain. It was only decades later that a schoolteacher called Peter Stuart Ney, lying on his deathbed in Rowan County, North Carolina, on 15 November 1846, confessed to his secret identity. He said he was Marshal Ney of France. The claim was thought at first to be preposterous, but the more that was discovered about Peter Ney's humble life in the United States, the more it seemed, well, just possible. In particular, Peter Ney was known to be a brilliant swordsman, so good that the fencing instructor for his students in nearby Mocksville told them they were in the presence of a master. The claim gathered momentum, so much so that Peter Ney's grave had to be turned into a secure mausoleum, to prevent it being smothered with kisses by Marshal Ney's American admirers.

But surely even Ney, handier with a sabre than a delicate rapier, could not have been so stupid as to hide his identity in the United States under his own name. There was no evidence that he had survived his execution in Paris, where an unidentified British cavalry officer, watching the proceedings, provoked outrage by leaping his horse over Ney's lifeless body.

(left) The execution of Marshal Ney. Within moments, an over-excited British cavalry officer foolishly leapt his horse over Ney's lifeless body.

IN MEMORY OF
PETER STEWART NEY
A NATIVE OF FRANCE
AND
SOLDIER OF THE FRENCH REVOLUTION
UNDER
NAPOLEON BONAPARTE
WHO DEPARTED THIS LIFE
NOVEMBER 15TH, 1846
AGED 77 YEARS

The brick mausoleum of Peter Ney in North Carolina

La Bédoyère, in contrast, faced a firing squad moved from its very public location in front of the Ecole Militaire to an obscure backwater on the plain of Grenville. Soldiers from the Tenth line regiment, the only one not to declare for Napoleon, were drafted in to form the firing party. They were told that all but one of their rifles was loaded with blanks. That was almost certainly untrue but whether they were all loaded, or none of them, no one can be sure. If Charles de la Bédoyère had been given heavy padding around his heart, told to play dead, and given two conflicting pieces of information about the number of real bullets coming in his direction, one thing seems certain. A man whose anatomy was protected in only one vital spot would certainly have been exhorting his comrades in arms, as he did, to shoot straight!

MON AMOUR POUR MON FILS

A PÛ SEUL

ME RETENIR À LA VIE!!....

———

ET C'EST LUI QUI M'A PRÉCÉDÉE.

(opposite) La Bédoyère is buried here in Paris - or is he?

Along with Oscar Wilde, la Bédoyère is buried in the Père Lachaise Cemetery in Paris. Unless that is, the American immigrant who claimed on his deathbed to be Marshal Ney simply took the surname of his greatest hero, unable completely to break with the past.

Georgine de Castellux had a young son to bring up but in normal circumstances, was far too valuable an asset for the Chastellux family to squander: she had become famous in her own right for the way she fought desperately for her husband's life. Even the Czar replied to her letters. Georgine never married again, although another marriage alliance was there for the taking. Unless of course, someone influential in the Chastellux family knew that Charles de la Bédoyère was not dead but living out the remainder of his life in complete obscurity, deep in the Carolinas, on the other side of the world.

Chapter Twelve

The Revenge of the Bathursts

THE FAMOUS PHILOSOPHER and economist, Adam Smith, in his *Theory of Moral Sentiments* (1759), was perhaps the first to postulate what became known as the Law of Unintended Consequences. When Castlereagh and Canning exchanged shots in a duel in September 1809, they could scarcely have imagined it would set in train a series of events that made certain that the world's most powerful man, Emperor Napoleon Bonaparte, would live out his last days on a remote island in the South Atlantic.

In March 1809, when Canning was looking for allies to unseat Castlereagh, he had struck a bargain with the trade minister, Lord Henry Bathurst. The earl promised his support in return for a plumb posting for his favourite 'nephew' (in fact the true relationship was more distant), 25-year-old Benjamin Bathurst, the third son of the Lord Bishop of Norwich - another Lord Henry Bathurst from a different branch of the family. So it came about that Benjamin, who had been residing with his wife and three young children as junior legate in humble Livorno, was suddenly given full ambassador status and sent to Vienna. His task was to detach Austria from the coalition that had closed all continental ports to British merchant shipping. No one expected him to succeed, but Benjamin set about the task with enterprise and tenacity. Austria did declare war on France, which ended in their disastrous defeat at Wagram in July. Bonaparte, furious with Britain in general and Benjamin in particular, demanded that the British Embassy in Vienna be closed and all its diplomats sent home.

Earl Bathurst: acting foreign minister, implacably opposed to any deal that allowed Napoleon to escape imprisonment

Benjamin Bathurst, who succeeded only too well in encouraging Austria to go to war with France

Benjamin, warned his life was at risk, would almost certainly have taken the safer, southern route back to London via the Adriatic, Trieste and Malta. However the forced resignations of Castlereagh and Canning left his benefactor, Earl Bathurst, in sole charge at the Foreign Office. The acting foreign minister, trying to make his mark, wanted Benjamin to return home via the Duchy of Mecklenburg and Hamburg. The British had intelligence that the governor of Mecklenburg would be willing to provide details of French troop movements on a regular basis for a substantial sum in gold coin.

Refused a safe conduct passport by Metternich, Benjamin decided to disguise himself as a German merchant, the Baron de Koch. As he was very tall, with blond hair and a moustache, this was not altogether successful. He travelled with William Krause, his German secretary, and a Swiss manservant.

The party set out on 9 November by coach and four from Budapest, where the Austrian court was in residence. They spent two uneventful days in Berlin. On 25 November they reached the Brandenberg town of Perleberg, halfway to Hamburg, but precariously close to the border with the French Confederation of the Rhine. Here Benjamin took rooms at the White Swan Inn, presumably intending to stay the night. It was perhaps an unwise choice, since Theodore Wagstaffe, a King's messenger, had been robbed of his dispatches not far from the same inn two years previously. In any event, Benjamin asked for an early supper. There are many conflicting accounts of what happened next but that was the last his companions saw of him.

After a few days, they decided to continue their journey to Hamburg and London, where the news of Benjamin's complete disappearance was received by the Cabinet with a mixture of incredulity and fury. Huge pressure was put on the Prussians to find Benjamin dead or alive. His expensive fur coat was discovered in the outhouse of the inn's ostler. Two weeks later, more ominously, the grey pantaloons he had been wearing were uncovered in nearby woods with two bullet holes in one leg but no signs of blood.

Within months the Prussians had Bathurst's formidable wife to contend with. Phillida was the daughter of Sir John Call, Baronet, a Cornish landowner. She arrived at Perleberg in March 2010, supported by the famous German explorer, Heinrich Röntgen, a family friend.

Phillida Bathurst: sometimes misidentified as her daughter, Rosa, who drowned aged 15 when her horse bucked in Rome and threw her into the river Tiber; but mother and daughter were uncannily alike.

Together they organised a search at prodigious expense of a vast area of surrounding forest by more than 100 men with dogs. Nothing was found. An acquaintance of Phillida in Magdeburg, wrote however to say that the governor, pointing to his fortress, had told her, 'They are looking far and wide for the English ambassador but I have him up there'. Röntgen confronted the governor, one of Napoleon's most devoted generals, Carra Saint-Cyr, who blandly informed him that the prisoner was someone else entirely.

General Count Carra Saint-Cyr, who imprisoned and probably killed Benjamin Bathurst

Phillida did not give up. She became almost the only British national during the Napoleonic wars to be granted a passport to Paris, where she was promised an audience with Bonaparte. When the French foreign office saw her list of questions for the Emperor, however, the audience was cancelled.

Corroborative evidence of the French involvement came from an unlikely source, Louis-Alexandre de Launay, comte d'Antraigues, a French secret agent. For a long time he basked in Napoleon's favour, turning a blind eye to Bonaparte's rumoured affair with the comte's lover and later wife, Antoinette de Saint-Humberty, a famous opera singer. D'Antraigues said that French troops abducted Benjamin from the inn and took him to Magdeburg, where the governor, on instructions from Fouché, interrogated then disposed of him.

Comte d'Antraigues,
a secret agent murdered in
London in 1812.
He knew what happened to
Benjamin Bathurst

Antoinette de Saint-Humberty was a famous opera singer, probably one of Napoleon's conquests. Her unwitting involvement in the dark arts of espionage led to her violent death in a leafy village outside London, known as Barnes, stabbed fatally through the breast

Röntgen met his death in mysterious circumstances near Timbuktoo three years later and the d'Antraigues suffered an even more dramatic fate. For their own safety they fled to England and set up residence in Barnes, near London. On 22 July 1812 the d'Antraigues had a ten o'clock appointment with Canning near Downing Street to give him a full account of the Benjamin affair and rose early. It was at that moment their Italian servant, Lorenzo, attempted to shoot the count with one of the four loaded pistols he kept by his bedside. When this failed, he stabbed both him and his wife fatally with a dagger. When the remaining servants attempted to seize him, Lorenzo shot himself with another of the count's loaded pistols.

In the Bathursts, led from the front by Phillida, Napoleon had made an implacable enemy. Earl Bathurst was the fiercest opponent of the proposition that Bonaparte could remain in power so long as France returned to her pre-1815 borders. Although numbered among prominent Whigs of the day, some of whom, even after Waterloo, supported the idea of allowing Napoleon to leave Europe for America, Bishop Bathurst may well have planted the seed of Napoleon's compulsory transfer to St Helena. He was certainly extremely well placed to do so. What is certain is that he nurtured the plant until its roots were resistant to the strongest winds of British and especially American pro-Bonaparte sentiment. Any hopes that Napoleon would be afforded another life in the New World were quickly extinguished.

A statue of Bishop Bathurst, who was always determined that Napoleon should be not be allowed to go to America

News, however sensational, travelled slowly beyond Europe. The outcome of Waterloo took six weeks to reach even the Eastern seaboard of the United States. On 31 July 1815 Captain Foster of the brig *Favorite* completed a 35-day crossing from Liverpool to Boston. He stepped ashore with a packet of English newspapers carrying Wellington's dispatch from the battlefield.

Americans by and large at first simply refused to believe it. When Captain Oxnard of the *Cora* followed the *Favorite* into Boston armed only with hearsay of a battle 'in which the French were victorious', the Boston *Patriot* seized upon it as gospel. It embellished the story in a report of how 'illuminations had been created in France, in consequence of the victory gained over Wellington'.

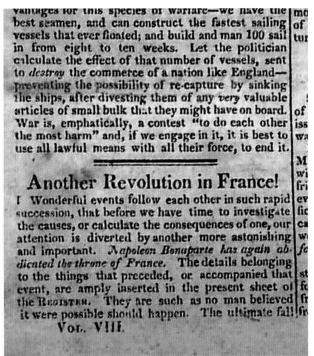

Napoleon abdicates again: the belligerent American press at first refused to believe the news coming out of Europe, then used it to try to rekindle hostilities with Britain. The American ambassador in Paris, the ailing Henry Jackson, having made himself look foolish by predicting victory for Bonaparte over the Allies, pressed the British government to give Napoleon a passport for the United States on his own authority. But then he could scarcely ask for instructions: it took twelve weeks for a diplomat's question to reach Washington and an answer to come back.

When the outcome ceased to be deniable, Americans were told by their press that Napoleon was 'about to embark, with a few faithful adherents, for the United States'. The story was given fresh oxygen when Captain Madge of the brig *Ludlow*, 40 days out of Bordeaux, was halted illegally on the high seas by an English frigate and 'strict search was... made over every part of the vessel' but nothing was found. For the *Pennsylvania Republican* published in Harrisburg, this was conclusive evidence that Napoleon 'intended to make his escape in some American vessel' and that the British Navy 'would search everyone they might fall in with to find the Emperor'. It was only on 23 August that optimism gave way to indignation with the news that Napoleon was destined for remote St. Helena. A New York leader said "Bonaparte was received less generously than felons transported to Botany Bay'.

On 28 November 1818, the mayor of Calais, said to be a fervent Bonapartist, held a dance at the town hall to celebrate 'the end of occupation by foreign armies'. He was a tad premature. When, towards midnight, the orchestra struck up a waltz, their melody was drowned out by the pipes and drums leading the 52nd Light Infantry, the last British troops in France. The curious waltzers made their way out into the street just in time to see the torn and tattered colours taken on board ship. It was the last leg of a journey that had begun badly for the regiment many years before in the Retreat from Corunna, when beating Napoleon had looked impossible. The best part of a century would pass before the British Army came back again.

Acknowledgements

The staff of the following, who showed endless patience:

The University of Oxford Faculty of History; the Bodleian Library, Oxford; the British Library; the London Library; the Bibliothèque of the Voltaire Institute in Geneva; the Austrian National Library, Hofburg Palace, Vienna; the Vienna University Library; the Royal Library of Belgium, Brussels; and four libraries in Paris: the Service Historique at Vincennes, the Bibliothèque Nationale, the Bibliothèque Sainte-Geneviève and the Bibliothèque de l'Arsenal.

And thanks also to:

John Armstrong, Laetitia Audumares, John Beare, Stéphane Bibard, Jean-Pierre Boudet, Stanislas Brugnon, comtesse Jeanne du Canard, Jan Colenbrander, Genna Gifford, Jill Hawksley, Camille Lebossé, Anthony Levi, Andrew Lownie, Sarah Macdonald, Claire Sauvrage, Catherine Walser and Diana Warwick.

Index

EUROPE
AFTER THE
CONGRESS OF VIENNA

English Miles

100 50 0   100   200   300

Faroe Is.

Bergen

Christ.

NORWAY

Scotland

Edinburgh

NORTH

DENMARK

Ireland

Dublin

SEA

Heligoland

HAMBURG

Holstein

Schleswig

Ems

Bremen

Lauenburg

HANOVER

Great Britain

Wales

England

London

Amsterdam

The Hague

Netherlands

Antwerp

Rhine

Scheldt

Brussels

Liège

Cologne

Aix la Chapelle

Mayence

Frankfort

Channel Is.

LUXEMBURG

Luxemburg

Meuse

Treves

Landau

Trier

CONF

BAV.

R. Seine

Paris

Orleans

Strassburg

Moselle

BADEN

WÜRTEMBERG

G.

Montbéliard

Basel

Constance

R. Loire

Neuchâtel

SWISS

Zurich

FRANCE

Bern

CONFEDERATION

Tyr

Saone

Geneva

Savoy

Trent

Lyons

Milan

Lombardo

Bordeaux

R. Rhone

Turin

Po

Guastalla

R. Garonne

Toulouse

Avignon

Piacenza

Parma

Genoa

Reggio

Nice

MONACO

Lucca

Marseilles

TUSC

Oporto

R. Douro

ANDORRA

Corsica

Elba

Ajaccio

R. Tib

PORTUGAL

SPAIN

Madrid

Barcelona

Lisbon

R. Tagus

Balearic Is.

Sardinia

Guadiana

R.

Valencia

Olivença

R. Guadalquivir

Seville

Granada

Cagliari

Tangier

Gibr.

MEDITE